A Heart at Peace

Kenneth J. Kremer

NORTHWESTERN PUBLISHING HOUSE
Milwaukee, Wisconsin

Cover Photos: Design Pics, Shutterstock
Art Director: Karen Knutson
Design Team: Pamela Dunn, Sarah Oberhofer

Northwestern Publishing House
1250 N. 113th St. Milwaukee, WI 53226-3284
www.nph.net

Published 2014
Printed in the United States of America
ISBN 978-0-8100-2600-1

To Ray

Contents

Acknowledgments

My sincere thanks to the more than 30 pastors who agreed to be interviewed during the conceptual stages of this project. Your candor reinforced the conviction that a new beginning in addressing conflict among God's people is desperately needed. I am likewise grateful for the clinical perspectives that Linda Reed and Rick Lowen contributed, as well as the thoughtful and constructive comments from individuals who read various drafts of the manuscript: Darin Aden, Charles Clarey, Robert Gurgel, Ronald Heins, Louis Meyer, Thomas Pankow, and the graduate students in my "Family Issues in Education" course. Your ideas have challenged and enriched my understanding of the issues.

A special tip-of-the-hat goes to my colleague Ray Schumacher. The project would have foundered without your constant encouragement.

Finally, I want to acknowledge the unwavering support of my dear wife, whose fresh and uplifting perspectives on biblical relationship-building are woven into the book's fabric. Marlis, I thank God every day for your wisdom and love.

From the Author

So there I was, sitting at a four-day peacemaking conference in Minneapolis, knowing that a coworker and I had been ramping up hostilities for more than a year. With a fresh commission in hand, I was trying to reconcile writing a book about *peacemaking* while hell-bent on destroying someone else's life. We were miserable warriors, she and I. But both of us were too stubborn to let a little thing like misery stop us from hating each other.

During the conference a colleague and I sat up late each night discussing my situation. He understood the irony. We considered Bible principles and weighed personal options. Practical strategies, however, eluded us. And real solutions seemed more distant than ever.

Three-and-a-half years later, the clichéd metaphor of *the journey* has thoroughly applied to this project. Writing *A Heart at Peace* has taught me some hard lessons—mostly about myself. Lessons like seeing enemies as human beings, forgiving and forgetting without conditions, loving patiently with compassion, mercy, gentleness, humility, acceptance, and respect. Along the way I've also learned to be a practical peacemaker.

My enemy's heart also changed. With the hope of God's promises and the power of his forgiveness, God healed our anger, salved our hurt pride, and repaired our damaged trust. We did not make it easy for him. Over time he replaced our at-war hearts with new attitudes that were beating to the rhythm of his own peace-loving heart.

On the same day that I put the finishing touches on this manuscript, the two former enemies enjoyed each other's company over lunch. We laughed and shed tears about the foolishness of our ill-advised feud. We acknowledged the remarkable miracle that God had worked in us. We recited prayers of confession, repentance, and thanksgiving. We told each other how much we treasured one another's friendship. We agreed to share our experience with others as evidence of the blessings we both have received through the peace and friendship of our new relationship.

Introduction

William Sherman—the celebrated Civil War Union Army general—said, "War is hell." He was right. Ask anyone who has experienced the heartache and suffering that conflict brings. When nations go to war, it can be hell. When family members loathe one another and work toward destroying one another, it is *hell.* When dissension and discord erupt within the church, *hell* is having its way. The gut-wrenching quarreling and fighting, the divorces and separations, the schisms and painful divisions that have occurred throughout the history of God's people bear ample testimony to the terrible destruction conflict causes. Today, in our homes, businesses, schools, service organizations, congregations, and mother church bodies, conflict wreaks havoc among God's people, leaving us with an acrid taste of the unending hatred that awaits unbelief in hell.

The good news is that the hellish war between God and his rebellious creatures is over. Peace has been restored. A divine love so pure and consistent with God's gracious nature drove him to slay[1] his dear Son on a battlefield outside the gates of a city called Peace.[2] It is on that battlefield that our struggle for securing a heart at peace with others begins. His love informs the conversation we are about to have. His grace compels us to explore the challenge of living in peace with one another and the hostile world beyond.

Some wars do more damage, cause more pain, or wreck more lives than others. Only a few are about defending noble causes; those battles are worth fighting. But in the main, conflict can rob us of the life God wants us to have, both here on earth and in eternity. The seeds of human conflict have the potential to destroy faith and bring souls to ruin. That is the underlying premise of this book.

When conflict threatened the congregation of believers in Corinth, the apostle Paul pleaded, "I appeal to you, brothers, in the name of our Lord Jesus Christ, that all of you agree with one another so that there may be no divisions among you and that you may be perfectly united in mind and thought. My brothers, some from Chloe's household have informed me that there are quarrels among you" (1 Corinthians 1:10,11). Paul understood that the fragile faith of some of the Corinthian believers was in grave danger because of the dissension and rancor simmering beneath the veneer of a false and uneasy peace.[3]

When Solomon wrote, "*A heart at peace* gives life to the body" (Proverbs 14:30), his point was that God created us for living lives of peace with one another. In God's worldview, living without peace is not really living at all. Unfortunately, the English word *peace* doesn't have the depth or range of a Hebrew *shalom.* With overtones of a greeting, a farewell, a blessing, a prayer, and even a binding contract, a Jewish shalom is packed with nuance. A heartfelt shalom can connote completeness, wholeness, health, peace, welfare, safety, soundness, tranquility, serenity, prosperity, satisfaction, rest, harmony, or the absence of agitation or discord. You and I have all of these in the special relationship we enjoy with our Lord Jesus. And while we wait patiently for his return, God wants us to live in peace with others. He wants this peace for us because it is for our good. Through commitment, hard work, and personal sacrifice, such earthly peace can sustain vibrant, healthy relationships between brothers and sisters, parents and children, friends, acquaintances, classmates, soul mates, marriage partners, extended family, business partners, and, yes, even between Christians and unbelievers. It plays a vital role in maintaining harmony and concord among fellow believers. Nevertheless, God also wants us always to remember that such temporal peace is completely eclipsed by that peace which Christ came to bring.[4] From the beginning it has always been God's desire to envelope humankind in his loving shalom. Yet the only world we have ever known is the world of struggle and tension, conflict and war, hatred and strife. It is impossible for us to imagine a time when the entire created universe was wrapped in unflawed tranquility. For people like us whose imaginations are clouded by the fog of sin, God inspired his prophet Isaiah to describe a return to Eden's transcendent peace.

> The wolf will live with the lamb,
> The leopard will lie down with the goat,
> The calf and the lion and the yearling together;
> And a little child will lead them.
> The cow will feed with the bear,
> Their young will lie down together,
> And the lion will eat straw like the ox.
> The infant will play near the hole of the cobra,
> And the young child put his hand into the viper's nest.
> They will neither harm nor destroy on all my holy mountain.
>
> ISAIAH 11:6-9

A haunting emptiness in all of us longs to be filled with God's holy shalom. But only in faith are you and I able to relate to Isaiah's surreal words.

For Adam and Eve, God's garden paradise was filled to overflowing with a satisfying and harmonious intimacy with their Creator. The profound peace of their conflict*less* existence[5] made such an idyllic life possible. They lived in unimaginable security.

Then their peace was shattered by sin. After safely securing Adam and Eve from the garden, God placed cherubim with a flaming sword[6]—an instrument of war—to guard the way to the tree of life.[7] Along with thorns, tears, and hard labor, conflict was now an integral part of the human experience. And without peace, life suddenly grew tenuous.

God's blueprint for overcoming sin's curse actually embraced conflict. The war that culminated on Golgotha's hill was a deadly war on a cosmic battlefield. The heel of the woman's Seed—the Messiah—was bruised. But her Seed crushed the serpent's head in the bloody clash. The resulting victory ushered in the divinely ordained peace between the loving Creator-God and his rebellious creatures. This was the only peace that ever really mattered—the transcendent peace that Jesus spoke of in John 14:27 when he reassured his disciples: "Peace I leave with you; my peace I give you. I do not give to you as the world gives. Do not let your hearts be troubled and do not be afraid." Christ's peace was precisely the kind of peace humankind needed.

After the fall, Yahweh's shalom echoed down through the long centuries that waited for his promise to be fulfilled. In the wilderness of Sinai, the Lord insisted that a shalom be spoken every day to his people as a special blessing: "The LORD bless you and keep you; the LORD make his face shine upon you and be gracious to you; the LORD turn his face toward you *and give you peace*" (Numbers 6:24-26). Here was solace for God's hungry, hurting, homeless nation. It gave hope to a beleaguered people who longed for peace at virtually every level of their meager existence. With these words the Lord *shalomed* his children day after wretched day with the good news that peace with him was already theirs in infinite abundance.

Two thousand years later, the planet that greeted the Lord's Prince of peace was eerily nestled in a span of history that is still remembered as the *Pax Romana* (the "Roman Peace"). Ironically, this brief global hiatus from war was stitched together with violence and brutality. Just months after the angels' hymn celebrating *peace on earth* had graced the Judean plains, Mary and Joseph were forced to flee to Egypt with their infant to escape the murderous hand of Herod the Great. In human flesh, God's Son was no stranger to conflict, even as a young child.

It was a reflective adult Jesus who bluntly observed, "In this world you will have trouble." His poignant words are as relevant today as they were when he said them. Notably, they were spoken in the context of peace: "I have told you these things, so that in me you may have peace. . . . Take heart! I have overcome the world" (John 16:33).

Overcoming the world meant that Christ would willingly expose himself to the lies of unbelievers, face the unjust judgments of evil men, suffer the ridicule of thugs, and endure a cruel and painful execution. Jesus knew what it was to be hated. When we think of the anguish and injustice he suffered at the hands of sinners like us, our hearts break. But we are also deeply grateful. The Savior's conflict on Calvary separated him from his Father's shalom in our place. Where you and I deserve to be cast out of God's loving presence and thrown into the furnace of everlasting war, his Son willingly and obediently stepped in as our substitute.

Because of Jesus and his redemptive work on our behalf, we can look forward to the eternal shalom that awaits us in heaven's glory.

But we still wait in a world where conflict is the norm and peace remains as ephemeral as ever. That is a problem. Worse, we are as engaged in the daily conflicts of life as our pagan neighbors. Jesus' prophetic declaration in Matthew 10:22 echoes down through the ages: "All men will hate you because of me." Because of Jesus, you and I are hated by a world that despises our Lord Jesus.

It is also true that most of us know what it is to hate others. What Christian hasn't experienced the disturbing emotions associated with a falling out with the boss, a moment of road rage, a bitter argument with a spouse, a fight with a bully on the playground, a raging quarrel with an in-law, a turf war at work, a savage confrontation on the church council, a flare of tempers with a parent, or a contentious charge filed in a court of law? We may recoil at the word, but if we are really honest, *hatred* describes exactly what is going on in our hearts during those times when things are not right in one of our relationships. And those times are many. And during those times, peace may seem to be an elusive specter, dancing out of reach (and almost out of sight) on some distant horizon.

A book about peace is necessarily about conflict's brutal impact on us all. A case study involving conflict at several different levels has been woven into the text. Its purpose is not to entertain but to teach, as is the purpose of the questions at the end of each chapter. They are there to provide a context in which we can see how Bible principles apply to us and our daily lives. The "Kids in Conflict" section (appendix A) and the "Five Smooth Stones" section (appendix B) were added later to help adults teach the basic Bible principles of Christian conflict resolution to the next generation of God's peacemakers.

Dealing effectively with conflict requires us first to look inward. In Part One we will examine the human heart to see how the sin that so often drives our conflicts causes us to behave as though we are at war. This can be a painful discussion—one that has the potential to bring each of us to our knees in humble repentance.

Part Two is aimed at helping us prepare for our co-mission. Jesus himself used the term *peacemaker* to describe a unique aspect of ministry.[8] Chapters 8 through 14 will look at conflict intervention from a gospel perspective, pondering the characteristics of a godly peacemaker and the tools God provides for doing such work. We will wrestle with the question of whether to approach group conflicts through internal intervention strategies or seek professional intervention from outside the organization. It is an important question that deserves discussion. We included it with the confidence that readers will understand there are several viable ways to approach intervention. The model provided is not introduced as the only solution or even the best solution. It is meant only to serve as a vehicle for offering a variety of ideas and suggestions.

In Part Three (chapter 15) we will turn our attention to the peacemaking work of Matthew chapter 28, where Jesus unleashes his army of believers (the church militant) into a holy battle to win lost souls for God's kingdom. Armed with the message of God's peace, this conversation will take us beyond the relatively safe environment of Christendom into the hostile milieu of an unbelieving world. It is the most noble of all battles. In the murky shadows of a world destroying itself in loveless conflict, a single truth emerges: *The only heart that truly knows peace is a heart purified in God's undeserved and unearned forgiveness.* While lost souls remain in contention, we have opportunities to explain the profound connection between *peace* on earth and *life* in Christ. On this battlefield, God gives purpose and meaning to our lives.

PART ONE

Christians in Conflict

Anyone who claims to be in the light but hates his brother is still in the darkness. . . . He does not know where he is going, because the darkness has blinded him.

1 JOHN 2:9,11

CHAPTER 1

Sin That Entangles

The Bible doesn't provide a lot of details in its account of the first human conflict. Moses (the author of Genesis) devoted only five sparse verses to a description of how Cain's felony went down. Moses' narrative leaves readers wondering why the account lacks the passion for such a brutal crime. It also leaves open questions about Cain's underlying motive and why he would kill Abel if he is really angry at God. The version that follows is admittedly a speculative account. Its purpose is to help us get a better grip on the reality of conflict and zero in our focus on conflict's sin-driven origin.

> *In the cool mist of a pristine dawn, a dark thread of smoke rose perpendicular against the burgundy horizon. Cain's brother was at it again, making a mockery of their clan's hardscrabble labors by wasting what little food there was on yet another sacrificial offering to the Lord Jehovah. "Oh, the stupidity," thought Cain, and he grieved over Abel's foolishness.*
>
> *For years Cain had brought his own token offerings of grain and vegetables to pay his respects. And he still did occasionally. Only, his heart was no longer as enthusiastic as the hearts of the others. His hard-earned offerings were aimed at winning the Deity's good will. But they seemed to go unappreciated.*

"If only Abel were less passionate about his worship," thought Cain. "Why must he openly flaunt his feelings for the Deity with these burnt sacrifices? . . . And why so often? Surely it is poor stewardship to render a prime animal into a heap of ashes. The healthy ones are the best breeders. Doesn't the Holy One desire that we first feed ourselves and meet the needs of our family?" With the authority of the firstborn, Cain felt duty bound to curb his brother's zeal and instruct him on the realities of their meager existence in a hostile world.

But something else, certain questions, irritated Cain. Why, for example, were Abel's offerings always accepted while his were not? How had he failed where Abel had succeeded? Was not the fruit of his labor just as worthy as Abel's? Lately Cain had even begun to wonder if Abel might be poisoning his relationship with the Almighty One. Had Abel somehow turned God against him? As a result, he harbored jealous thoughts over the intimacy his brother enjoyed with the Lord. At the same time, Cain wondered to himself if Abel's God was really worthy of all the attention; after all, it was he, Cain, who lived by the sweat of his own brow. He survived day-to-day by his own cunning and the skills he had developed. If he prospered, it was by his own hand; if he failed, he would have only himself to blame.

As Cain stormed off in the direction of Abel's sacrifice, the Lord whispered truth to him one final time—a merciful warning: "Beware! Sin, like a wild beast, is crouching nearby, taut and ready to attack. You are its intended prey."

Yahweh's words left no impression. Cain had already made up his mind. It was his duty to shape the will of his younger sibling, to impress upon Abel that he, Cain, was the elder and therefore knew what was best. If Abel was unwilling to listen, he was prepared to be forceful, to draw a line in the sand. His brother needed to understand that the first law of survival in a sin-ridden world is the law of strength, power, leverage, and brute force.

And Abel did resist. He had other ideas about what was important—priorities that his brother would never understand. From Abel's perspective, Cain trusted too much in his own cunning. For Abel, a relationship with the Lord God was far more important than any other thing. After all, it was God who fed him and the other members of his household, clothed them, sheltered them, protected them. How could he live without worshiping his infinite provider? How else would he express his appreciation for the merciful Creator's plan to make everything right and good again?

The brothers argued. Cain's angry words filled Abel with sadness. Abel's gentle and submissive posture only angered Cain all the more. Soon Cain was consumed by a white-hot rage that demanded more than angry words. "Come," he invited, "walk with me across this meadow so that we can resolve our differences." But Cain's intent was to deceive Abel instead of reconciling their dispute. He knew that while his brother's posture might have been submissive, Abel would never submit to his will. It was time to take firm action.

When Cain was sure no one else could see, he picked up a jagged rock and struck his brother's skull from behind—with full force. As Abel's broken body slumped to the ground with a heavy thud, Cain was pleased. The dark red liquid pumping rhythmically from the gaping wound in his brother's skull meant that his brother was not going to get up to fight back. Abel was dead.

Cain had helped his father slaughter many animals; he understood death. But this was the first time Cain had seen the death-curse happen to a fellow human being. It made him sick enough to retch. Life is a precious thing. But Cain was not sorry this had happened. "Now," thought Cain, "at least the others will know that I am the elder and the wiser. Abel should have listened to me when he had the chance." And Cain's heart became as hard as the bloodstained rock in his hand.

Though the account of Cain murdering Abel in Genesis chapter 4 may be terse and lacking passion, it also has the makings to be one of the Bible's most gripping narratives. It has a great plot; plenty of violence; deception and intrigue; a likeable, innocent victim; a coldhearted villain; dramatic tension; and conflict. Kids love it. They don't see the sad implications this story has for every man, woman, and child who ever walked the planet.

Adults understand. We have seen the path of destruction that sin leaves in its wake. We have real-life experiences with the bitter taste of conflict. Cain's brutal attack on his brother reminds us of the dark ideas that can infest our own hearts—ideas that can even lead to murder. No, this event was not recorded for the purpose of holding the reader's attention raptly with a well-spun tale. God's Spirit moved Moses to record it for a very good reason. You and I are supposed to learn something from it. So, what is it that we are supposed to learn?

Cain's attack on Abel reminds us of the dark thoughts that can infest our own hearts.

When scholars read this, many see this account as a necessary part of the larger story line of Scripture. They say that it is important for making sense of everything else that follows—the rest of the Bible, or even the rest of human history. They see it as a bridge that takes us from the first sin to the truth about all the succeeding generations (including ours and those that will follow us), all plagued with the same impure thoughts and selfish motives that were passed along from Adam and Eve to Cain and Abel and the rest of us that followed. These scholars are, of course, right. The story of Cain and Abel tells us something about ourselves.

Others argue that this is the first example of how sin affected our relationships with one another—proof that sin not only destroyed our relationship with the Creator but did untold damage to the way we interact with one another. They are also correct.

Lutheran theologians like to assert that this is a lesson aimed at teaching us about God's mercy and love, even for an unbeliever like Cain. And it is clearly that. We will pick up that thread in later chapters when we discuss conflicts between believers and unbelievers.

A Question of Identity

For the majority of us, however, these unsettling verses often boil down to one very important question: *With whom do I identify—Abel, the innocent victim, or Cain, the murderous villain?* Note, the question is not *With whom do I sympathize?* Most sympathize with Abel. He didn't deserve to be murdered. We all agree on that. No, the question is more about how we see ourselves. Are we more like Cain, who has evil thoughts passing through his mind that he can't, or won't, control? Or do we see ourselves as Abel, the poor schlep who gets whacked for being a decent, God-fearing person? It's a great way to begin our discussion about conflict, because no matter which direction you are inclined to lean, your answer has the potential to tell you a lot about yourself.

None of us cares to think of himself or herself as a murderer. Nevertheless, there are at least a few people in every crowd who will immediately identify with Cain. They recall a relationship in which they have fantasized about *erasing* a certain individual who perennially makes their life miserable. Now they feel guilty for having entertained such hateful thoughts.

Do you identify with Cain? Have you ever really hated someone?

On the other hand, many Bible readers will see themselves walking in Abel's sandals—the bystander who doesn't deserve to be drawn into a fight. There is a little self-righteousness in this position. Those who identify with Abel may also feel justified in hissing and booing all the murderous villains who have ever lived—Attila the Hun, Adolf Hitler, Jack the Ripper, Osama bin Laden, and all the rest.

It is always interesting to debate this Cain-or-Abel proposition. Some people actually become quite passionate as they defend one position or the other. Of course, it's a trick question. In the end, you and I need to identify with *both* Cain *and* Abel.

Sometimes we really are innocent victims—walking the strait and narrow, taking the high road, minding our own business. In spite of our innocence, we may still get dragged into a war that is not of our own making. But there are other times when we are responsible for doing untold damage to another person because we *started it,* or *prolonged it,* or *finished it* in a way that caters to our darker (read that *sinful*) desires.

Martin Luther described the Christian's dual nature as a constant battle between the *old* (sinful) *Adam* (sometimes also called the *old man*) and the *new man* modeled after Christ Jesus. Luther saw the new man emerging as the dominant force, the result of God's Spirit working through Word and sacrament. But Luther also recognized that while we remain in this life, the old Adam will continue to be a problem. He said that the old, sin-driven self needs to be *drowned in daily repentance.* That's interesting language—*conflict language.* Drowning, especially drowning under someone's deadly grip, is a violent way to die. Yet Luther argued that our old Adam needs to be put down regularly, emphatically, often, and in a violent manner so that it does not get a toehold on a Christian's life and overwhelm him or her with all sorts of vices and temptations.

The Conflict Within

A very real conflict is still going on in each one of us between our old Adam and our new man in Christ. The battle is being waged all the time. This is a good reason for being careful about picking our battles. A noble cause is certainly worth going to war over. Jesus fought a noble battle against the self-righteous hypocrisy of the Pharisees. Of course, Jesus is God's Son—a perfect and righteous person. His conflicts were always righteous. Sinners like us would only be fooling ourselves to think that all of our conflicts are truly as altruistic and honorable as the ones Jesus fought. In fact, the opposite is more likely to be true. Most of the battles you and I wage are aimed at serving ourselves. We may do a good job of masking our underlying purposes, but upon closer examination, we are likely to discover that ego and self-will have had a lot of influence in our battles.

Understanding this sinner/saint (old Adam/new man in Christ) nature of every Christian is especially helpful for understanding conflict. No matter how you slice it, all Christians are in the same boat in at least this one respect: We are all works in progress.[9] But because Christ Jesus has taken up residence in our hearts and the power of God's Holy Spirit is working in our lives, the saintly new man is in control . . . most of the time.

On the other hand, our new man in Christ may not always be in control. (And here's the sticking point.) When conflict strikes and we engage the enemy, the likelihood that our new man will be able to remain in charge decreases.

You've heard of the phenomenon that adversely affects decisions made in the heat of war. Military experts refer to this as the *fog of battle.* Well, this mysterious syndrome has a spiritual parallel that kicks in whenever we are engaged in the heat of a spiritual battle. Even without the element of hatred, our spiritual perspective can easily become confused under battle conditions. In the environment of conflict, the old man sees an opening for putting himself back in the driver's seat. Just when we need to keep our eyes focused on Jesus, we tend to stop following his model and revert back to our old-Adam instincts.

In his book on Christian conflict resolution, Alfred Poirier writes, "We must understand that the conflicts people are in are conflicts in people—conflicts of desires, demands, and idols. These are true strongholds that are impregnable except through the gospel of Jesus Christ. And it is this gospel that we were called to preach and teach."[10] While you and I zealously confess our faith in the Lord Jesus and his saving gospel, we are far from having immunity from this world's conflicts. Even when we are trying to help other Christians work through their personal conflicts,[11] we must be aware of the dark and ugly things that Christians are capable of thinking and doing when driven by their old Adam. And we need to apply that same awareness to ourselves, lest we become tangled up in some of the same sins.[12]

A Disturbing Fact of Life

This concept that we are still vulnerable to Satan's conflict trap is sometimes hard for Christians to swallow. But it's true. You and I don't always live as God wants us to. And when we are not behaving as God's children, we are prone to getting caught up in a culture that lives and breathes conflict. At the very least, *sin lies at the door.* Because we are both old Adam and new man in Christ, we can still be deceived by sin's deadly allure. When that happens in an environment filled with tension, bitterness and rage can finally bubble to the surface in full-blown, white-hot hatred. Wrongful attitudes and emotions give way to sinful behaviors and actions. And we stop behaving as members of God's family and start behaving like children of the devil.

Perhaps you are saying to yourself, *"But I go to church every week, pray every day, read the Bible with regularity. I don't go around picking fights with people."* Some of Jesus' disciples held a similar view. Like us, they too were works in progress. Sometimes their failures and shortcomings were rather glaring. On the night when Jesus was bound and dragged away like a common criminal, the fog of battle set in for Peter, and soon he was slashing away at his enemies with a sword.

The author of the general letter to the Hebrews wrote, "Therefore, since we are surrounded by such a great cloud of witnesses, let us throw off everything that hinders and the sin that so easily entangles, and let us run with perseverance the race marked out for us. Let us fix our eyes on Jesus, the author and perfecter of our faith" (12:1,2).

The "great cloud of witnesses" in the early part of that verse is referring to the many heroes of faith who appeared throughout the Old Testament. Abel is mentioned, along with Enoch, Noah, Abraham, Isaac, Jacob, Joseph, Moses, and a few others. The lives of these people stand as models for Christians like us. We've learned about many of them in Sunday school or sitting at the feet of a God-fearing parent or grandparent. All of them were works in progress. Almost all of them had to deal with conflict at some time in their lives. But with God's strength, they persevered. With the examples of these great men and women of faith to guide us, we need to cast off those sins that threaten to ensnare us.

There are, of course, lots of ways to become entangled in sin—sex, drugs, greed, a craving for power. The list is long and daunting. But one way stands out. It was the reason given in Scripture for God's utter destruction of all living things at the time of the great flood (Genesis 6:11): violence and conflict. Conflict is a veritable web of temptations that can involve all of the other vices that man's sinful imagination might follow.[13] And wherever conflict threatens, sin is crouching at the door; it desires to have us. With God's help, we must learn to master it.[14]

For Thought and Discussion

- How do we go about the grim business of daily drowning our old Adam?
- Why are we more vulnerable to temptation when we are caught up in a conflict?
- As God's *works in progress*, what thoughts regarding conflict could be included in our daily prayers?

CHAPTER 2

Predictable Patterns

Big storms are common along the Atlantic Seaboard. Old salts call them *nor'easters*. In 1991, early in the last week of October, a nor'easter named Hurricane Grace skipped along the coast, skirting the Bahamas. By midweek a second cyclonic depression had slipped down the coast from Nova Scotia to join forces with Grace. Sometime on October 30, the two systems merged about 100 miles off Cape Cod. Later that same day, the newly formed system, which was never officially named a hurricane, collided with a monster high-pressure ridge of cold Canadian air swooping in from the Midwest. The result was a weather system so large and powerful that it deserves a place in history all its own. A television broadcaster dubbed it "the perfect storm." Sebastian Junger later wrote a best seller using the newsman's phrase as his title. The story tells of the tragic loss of the *Andrea Gail,* a 72-foot fishing vessel that went down somewhere in the North Atlantic in gales of more than 100 knots and waves that have been calculated at over 100 feet.

In spiritual terms, conflict is the perfect storm of sinful entanglements. And just as meteorologists analyze patterns in nature that combine to create powerful weather systems, a study of the anatomy of a developing conflict can be very instructive.

Like weather systems, conflicts often follow a predictable course. Fortunately, a lot of groundbreaking work has already been done in the area of conflict. In fact, some findings are almost two thousand years old. Yet the insights of one author in particular resonate fresh, as if his words were rendered just yesterday. The writer's name was James. He was an apostle and the man who composed the general New Testament epistle with the appropriate title "James." James had a special talent for understanding people—especially people involved in conflict. His short letter in Scripture has much to say about human relationships and the heartrending conflicts we endure. Writing in terms that are disarmingly personal, James analyzed the pattern for a growing conflict. His target audience consisted of folks like us—sinner-saints. The question he posed is what interests us in this chapter: "What causes fights and quarrels among you?" (James 4:1).

Saint James was never one to beat around the bush. He approached his topic with a searing rhetorical question. And he didn't waste time getting right to the heart of the matter with an answer: "Don't [fights and quarrels] come from your desires that battle within you? You want something but don't get it. You kill and covet, but you cannot have what you want. You quarrel and fight. You do not have, because you do not ask God. When you ask, you do not receive, because you ask with wrong motives, that you may spend what you get on your pleasures" (James 4:1-3).

Forceful words. Did you feel their impact? Some would say James crossed the rudeness line when he indicted every member of his reading audience. With the icy finger of accusation, James said it's all because of *your* desires that conflicts arise—all of you. *You* want. *You* kill. *You* covet. *You* do not have because *you* have wrong motives. You. YOU! *You* are the problem. The fights and quarrels you get tangled up in originate in the darkness of *your* own heart. What's more, the root cause of it all is that *you want.*

So how accurate was the apostle? If you and I are completely honest, we'd admit he was spot-on. The human heart is the very first place to begin looking for the causes of conflict. Each of us needs to honestly assess the motives in our own hearts before we lay blame at the feet of someone else. My own sinful self could very well be an integral part of the nasty conflict I am fighting.

The Seeds of Conflict

This is about the time when most of us, dear reader, get up on our high horses in protest to challenge the notion that there may be something wrong with wanting something—with dreaming big. After all, in one way or another, we each subscribe to the concept of the great American dream. Disney built an empire based on the idea that our dreams can come true if we just wish hard enough. For humankind, dreams are a default setting—a given. When the harsh realities of life hit us the hardest (think of the worst things that can happen), we still dream. So what's wrong with that?

Actually, the objects of our wanting aren't that important. James didn't even bother to cite examples. Nor was he saying that there is anything inherently wrong with wanting or even dreaming big. He was saying that if you are searching for the seeds of conflict, look no further than your own heart. That's where ungodly desires can put down tiny shoots that eventually root and spring up as full-blown, hate-filled, smashmouth conflicts. He was saying that even our dreams are tainted.

Let me be the first to offer up a *mea culpa:* There are things *I want.* Isn't that true for everyone? We'd have to be unconscious not to want. I'll even admit there are a few things I am willing to fight for. And I have some ideas about what others may want bad enough to fight for as well. Some of our desires (for example, power, fame, influence, money, etc.) have the potential to corrupt even the most pious disciple. It's easy to label these longings as dangerous. On the other hand, a good education, responsible government, reasonable health, freedom, a loving spouse, servant-minded pastors and teachers, God-fearing children, a satisfying job, and loyal friends are definitely worth dreaming about. We may even refer to them as *blessings*. We teach our children to vigorously pursue them. Should we feel guilty for wanting these blessings?

And what about those things we unselfishly want for others? A meaningful life. A stronger faith. Another day of grace. Is that so wrong?

The problem with characteristic old-Adam thinking is that our wanting can degenerate into self-serving obsessions. And when we put self at the center of our wanting, it can become idolatrous. Alfred Poirier explains how in the heart of a sinful person, even God-pleasing intentions can become idolatrous:

> Most of the time our desires are good. They turn bad when we start *serving* them—when we treat them as gods and they rule over us. . . . The evil is not what we want but in wanting it too much. It is not in the desire but in making the desire an ultimatum (when only God is ultimate, and only God should give ultimatums). . . . As counterfeit gods, idols are lawgivers. They command us. They shape our affections, direct our decisions, and motivate our behavior. What we do we do because we obey the command of our [false inner] god.[15]

Godly wanting always lines up with God's holy will. It echoes Jesus' prayer: "Your will be done."[16] It approaches the Father's throne with motives driven by our faith in Jesus. Such wanting is in complete harmony with the compassion we see in his life and death.

Self-serving obsessions have a way of replacing God's will with my will. That's a significant shift. We dare not let it go unnoticed. A *self-serving obsession* is the very first stage of a conflict in the making.

In his gospel, Mark recorded a revealing little episode involving two brothers who had come to know Jesus well. Their names were James and John. For two-and-a-half years they had followed Jesus everywhere, sitting at his feet, drinking in the many wonderful lessons he taught, witnessing his incredible miracles. One day, when they had gathered up the nerve, the two brothers came to Jesus with a request. "Teacher," they began, "*we want* you to do for us *whatever we ask*" (Mark 10:35). How blatant can self-indulgent wanting be? Even when we try to put their request in the best possible light, it's difficult to find much of a "Your will be done" attitude in those words.

Have you ever prayed with the attitude James and John had? I have. A reasonable guess is that most of us have. Our wanting is often spoiled by self-serving attitudes. Our underlying motives are not always as righteous as we may like to believe.

From Self-Serving Obsession to False Perception

Our self-serving obsessions have an adverse effect on how we see the world we live in. Wanting something so badly shapes our view of the truth. Wrongheaded desires inevitably distort our understanding of reality and fact.

Such *distortions* mark the second stage in a growing conflict. Journalists call it *spin.* Spin inevitably leans in our favor, sometimes in very subtle ways. Twisted truth is not really truth at all. And you don't have to be a journalist to operate a spin machine. We are all predisposed (by sin) to a version of the *truth* that is undergoing constant revision. All of it is designed to protect the self-serving obsession that has quietly grown into a little idol, secretly hidden in a dark place within the heart.

Twisted truth is not really truth at all.

Judge and Jury

Judging is the third phase. When I am no longer able to discern objective truth, it is really quite easy to see the flaws and faults of others, even as I see myself as flawless and innocent. The old Adam uses this ploy to get us to concentrate on the weaknesses and sins of others when we should be focusing on our own. As judge, I can rearrange the furniture of my own sins so that the sins of the person I am judging will always appear more heinous than my own. Or, perhaps, I will simply ignore my own defects and blemishes altogether.

The judging phase has some other interesting overtones. If I am the judge, I can also convince myself that I am effectively eliminating the possibility that the person I am judging will do the same to me. It's flawed logic, and we all know it's not true. Nevertheless, we still want to believe that when we judge others, we are taking away their power to judge us.

Head Executioner

The fourth and final stage of a developing conflict is the most observable. It is the stage in which the judge carries out the *punishment.* If open hostilities haven't already broken out from growing tensions, this phase is usually potent enough to incite open warfare.

In a sense, the punishing stage is merely an extension of the judging stage. As judge, I not only declare guilt but I also *determine punishment.* Nevermind that my authority as another person's judge is self-declared or that my view of another person's guilt is the result of some twisted view of the truth.

Punishing another person can involve little more than a disapproving glance or the flip of a simple gesture. But it can also be as severe as the punishment Cain brought down on Abel. In any case, the intent is to exact a penalty that is thinly veiled as justice.

The punishing phase brings a kind of unholy closure to the whole cycle. My obsessive desire has now shifted. My new obsession is to destroy the enemy who has dared to stand in my way of securing my own obsession. To that end I have accepted the lie that tells me I have the moral authority to pursue my new desire. Using the authority this lie convinces me I have, I conclude that my enemy is unquestionably guilty. My moral obligation is to carry out the sentence without any consideration for due process or mercy. End of story.

If you're on the receiving end of someone's intent to serve as your judge, jury, and head executioner, you have a real sense of how troubling this final stage can be. We rebel against the injustice of trumped-up charges served up in kangaroo courts by self-appointed judges. It's just not fair! The code of the jungle calls for a response; and wherever there is injustice, there is fuel for a raging conflict.

The model for a gathering conflict, then, has four distinguishable phases: *I (we) obsess. I (we) distort. I (we) judge. I (we) punish.* Without intervention, each phase will inevitably drive the hearts of sinners toward conflict. Some conflicts follow the pattern in lockstep manner. Some people get stuck for a while in one of the early phases. Some people change the order or combine stages in ways that make them more difficult to observe. Serious disputes all seem to have at least one thing in common: The pattern gathers momentum, grows in intensity, and eventually entangles more people, resulting in dysfunction.

For Thought and Discussion

- Can knowing the pattern for a developing conflict help deter or undo it?

- Read Matthew 5:44. Then develop a simple test that could be used to determine if a Christian's motives over and against an enemy are God-pleasing.

- Many of the Bible's narratives document conflict in various stages of development. One of the most fascinating is recorded in Genesis chapter 16, where a tangled assortment of *obsessive, distorted, judgmental,* and *punishing* behaviors is documented. This tangled web of conflict tore Abram's family apart and ruined several people's lives. Read this account of conflict and dysfunction. Look for examples of each of the four phases of conflict.

A Case Study

We read Genesis chapter 1 with jaw-dropping awe, scratching our heads at the intricacy and vastness of our universe and searching for a vocabulary to express our wonder. When words fail us, God provides the words of an inspired writer (Moses) to put creation's super-miracles into perspective. Like the peal of a cosmic bell, Moses repeats the same proclamation seven times within the space of 31 verses: It is *good, good, good, good, good, good;* it is all *very good.* Then, like a lightning bolt that startles the night sky, two words trump everything that has been reported so far: Something is *not good* (Genesis 2:18).

Don't despair! The Maker hasn't suddenly detected a flaw. The story line is about to take an exciting new direction. The unexpected *not good* introduces an even more wonderful dimension of the Godhead. We are about to learn that the Maker's heart beats to the rhythm of a boundless love for his own dear, image-bearing creature.

So what is this *not good* thing that demands our undivided attention? It is the state of complete and utter *aloneness. It is not good for the human being to be alone.* This is God conversing with God, committing himself to a fundamental concept—one that reveals a vital truth about his most intimate personal being; humankind will be a relational creature because our three-in-one God is a relational being. The human heart is (more properly, *was*) like the heart of its Maker. Even in our imperfect state we love because our Creator loves. It would not be good if a person could not love his friends, parents, children, spouse, and colleagues. That would be hell. So God fashioned the first human relationship. Before Adam and Eve were the first society, the first family, the first marriage, or even the first church, they represented the first human relationship. Ever since, the human experience has been inexorably bound to the relationships we have with one another. Remarkable, is it not? Our relationships—what a wonderful gift!

On the other hand, if you're naïve enough to believe that we will consider every relationship to be a wonderful gift, then you haven't heard about some of *my* relationships. Or perhaps you've forgotten about some of your own.

In a world that no longer resembles Eden's tranquility, too many of our God-given relationships have ended up on the dung heap of heartache and disappointment. No wonder the notion of living on some tiny, deserted island in the Pacific is so appealing! We are like the traveling salesman who observes that the town he is visiting would be a veritable paradise, if only it were not for the wretched people living in it. Truth is, our relationships have been so badly distorted by sin that their wonderful qualities as divine gifts are barely recognizable. We may even tend to think of at least some of our relationships as more of a curse. Yet you and I have very little choice in the matter. Having relationships with other people is not an option; we are created to be relational beings.

That said, the disappointments we may have regarding some of our personal relationships could probably use some sanctified tempering. God still chooses people—flawed, cracked, and broken vessels that we are—to carry living water to those who are dying in unbelief.

That doesn't happen without relationships. He uses our relationships to plant seeds, train the young, correct the straying, and lift up the weak. How dare we disdain his gift? How dare we fail as stewards of this precious gift by allowing peace and unity to deteriorate into hatred and enmity?

As out of sync with truth this disdain and failure may seem, our lives are marred by the evidence of their presence. And the evidence is often all too fresh. The story of an imaginary conflict in an imaginary church will remind us that we can't claim innocence. It will remind us of just how real and dangerous our failures are.

Welcome to Peace Lutheran Church

Peace Evangelical Lutheran Church is a congregation of about 450 souls. Its history stretches back to the 1880s. Every member knows the story of the night in 1967 when lightning struck the bell tower of the original building. The 65-year-old frame structure burned to the ground in less than an hour. Bitter infighting followed. Half the congregation wanted to rebuild on the site where the old church once stood. The other half thought it more prudent to relocate near the new highway at the edge of town. The first group carried the day by a single vote. Old-timers privately have their own suspicions about how that vote went down.

For almost a century, Peace has owned and operated its own elementary school. In years past, enrollment always hovered somewhere between 100 and 120 children. Then, about ten years ago, enrollment began to decline steadily.

To shore up the ministry program, Peace added a child care program. This program has had limited success in reaching out to the community. Some members consider the child care program a financial burden. For the last few years, it has been necessary to dip into an endowment fund to keep the program afloat. The detractors are quick to point out that this cannot go on indefinitely.

Peace Evangelical Lutheran Church is located in Mount Powell, an amiable midwestern town of almost 40,000 people. A mix of small industry, small businesses, and two large insurance companies headquartered outside of town contribute to a stable economy. In spite of Mount Powell's prosperity, many of the older homes in the church's immediate neighborhood have fallen into disrepair, and a demographic change is taking place. Yet this shift is not reflected in the church's mission-vision plan.

Church attendance could be better. Bible class attendance has fallen off. The Sunday school program is nearly defunct. Teen programs come and go. Outreach projects are generally ill conceived and poorly organized. Follow-up is spotty at best.

The graying of the congregation is another growing concern. The school manages to attract enough new families to provide some hope for the future. In spite of its declining enrollment, many members see the school as the congregation's only hope for survival. Others quietly wonder if the congregation should consider new directions that will not depend so heavily on the costly venture of operating a parochial school.

Two years ago a handful of members proposed closing the school. The idea never generated much traction. But it did raise a few eyebrows. Undaunted, the group refined their rationale and ramped up the rhetoric. A few individuals got carried away and said some things that should not have been said. Soon the battle lines were drawn, and folks on both sides became guilty of loveless words and hurtful behaviors.

Several families transferred to another congregation across town. Their reason for making such a move was the discordant atmosphere at Peace. But they were careful with whom they shared that perspective and with what they said. A few others quietly hinted that they would be curtailing their financial support for the school. Still others argued that the child care program should be abandoned. The mission of carrying out a gospel ministry at Peace Lutheran Church came to a virtual standstill. Church meetings centered on the obvious impasse; without any hope for resolution, dialog became gridlocked with poor information and faulty logic. Outside of church, members talked or argued about church issues and church politics. Peace Lutheran Church was steadily slipping into a cold war.

Most organizations—including businesses, schools, churches, and families—can become a stew pot of simmering issues. There's a good explanation for this: Conflict is all about people and their relationships. It sounds silly to say it in this way; of course conflict is about people. Still, it's an important fact to acknowledge . . . and to keep on acknowledging. We tend to forget: While circumstances may have a lot to do with increased tensions, it is people who make choices about how they will respond. A budgetary shortfall doesn't become a major issue until people get the notion that there's a problem with someone else's calculations, giving habits, or fiscal integrity. A school can't cause a turf war unless people begin to have different views about its value, its purpose, or how it can be managed more efficiently. Even the strong opinions people have about how their offerings will be spent cannot disrupt the peace until the people begin to act on those opinions in a way that threatens or demeans the opinions of others. It's *people* who obsess over what they want. It's *people* who distort the truth to suit their own self-serving purposes. It's *people* who judge one another. And it's *people—sinful people*—who take it upon themselves to punish others with hateful words and mean-spirited behaviors. Human conflict could not exist without people. Knowing what drives people into conflict is paramount.

Differences of Opinion

Ned Constantino is the chairman of the Spiritual Growth Committee at Peace. He is not afraid to speak his mind but generally embraces the *iron-sharpens-iron* principle.[17] For Ned it is not a bad thing for people to disagree. Like a lumberjack grinding the edges of two iron axe heads together, he believes that two conflicting ideas can eventually sharpen each other and lead to a much-improved solution. Ned recognizes that there are many matters in which God has given us the freedom to make a choice.

We may not always agree, but when we are careful to listen to those who disagree with us, we learn. We begin to see our options from a new angle. We get to know one another. We *relate.* And because we are followers of our Lord Jesus, we relate to one another in ways that will lovingly build one another up in the faith.[18]

But differences of opinion do not always lead to a stronger consensus or a deeper unity. Some differences lead to conflict, especially if they are accompanied by attitudes that refuse to listen to the perspectives of others. The members of Peace Lutheran Church know one another well. But their differing views seem to be tearing the congregation apart. That's a strong indication that many of them have already become entrenched in their positions.

Trust and Mistrust

Mark Eastman, the chairman of the Christian Education Committee at Peace, isn't so sure that iron always sharpens iron. Mark and his erstwhile business partner, Stan Moralis, who is also a member of Peace and currently the president of the congregation, have been bitter enemies for several years.

In the early 1990s, Mark and Stan built a successful travel agency together. When the travel industry took a left turn, some bad business decisions were made. Mark and Stan declared bankruptcy. They still blame each other, taking turns at charging each other with bad-faith deals and dishonest business practices. They both believe the other is dishonest. Stan actually filed suit against Mark about a year ago. He dropped the suit only because he didn't think he could prove his claim in a court of law.

Mark would prefer to put the painful rift with Stan in the past, but he has difficulties with the way Stan carries out his duties as president of the congregation. From Mark's perspective, there are just too many secret meetings and unreported decisions at church. He is convinced that Stan intentionally misleads and deceives other men on the church council and the members in general. He suspects that Stan isn't being entirely forthright in telling members what's going on behind the scenes. Mark is pretty sure that Stan has a hidden agenda—one that seeks the closing of both the school and the child care center. He bluntly refers to Stan's approach as *dirty* church politics.

Mistrust ignites more conflict than any other cause. Even when there are other mitigating origins for a conflict, suspicion is frequently hiding in the background. At some level, all serious conflict is about the truth and how people interpret it. And as a general rule of thumb, most individuals assume their enemies are completely lacking in integrity.

The three-legged stool of the Lutheran Reformation bases all of the church's teachings on three fundamental assertions: *sola fide* (Latin for "by faith alone"), *sola Scriptura* ("by Scripture alone"), and *sola gratia* ("by grace alone").

Our faith in God and his ever-abiding promises to redeem us rests on the assumption that God is telling us the truth in his revealed Word. Without that, you and I have no hope. Our relationship with God has value only if (1) he is telling us the truth and (2) we believe what he says. Given the importance of truth, then, we shouldn't be too surprised to find that Scripture is bursting with references to honesty and integrity—both God's and ours.

If our relationship with God rests entirely on whether he is telling us the truth, we can also conclude that our relationships with others will likewise need to be anchored in the confidence that others place in our words. Even in the secular world of business and commerce, no one would be able to function without an element of trust (at the very least, trust in a signed contract). One would hope that the Christian community would at least rise above the standards set by secular enterprise. Unfortunately, that is not always the case.

The apostle Paul addresses the matter of truth and trust by pointing out that the things we say to others (or write to others) should be a reflection of our Savior's truthfulness and integrity. He starts, then, at the very highest level of communication, citing the gospel as the ultimate truth-message that anyone could ever convey. This divine truth is itself living; and it gives life to all who believe it.[19]

The eternal futures of souls, purchased and won with holy blood, depend on the integrity of God's Word and how it is shared among us. God's people—the church—cannot allow false teachings to stand among us unchallenged because false teachings (and the false teachers who promote false teachings) put people's faith at risk. At the same time, our personal lives must rise above the world's standards for integrity.[20] For Christians, it is not enough to be honest up to a point; God wants us to be honest to a fault. Deception of any kind can undermine the confidence people have in the things we say to them about Jesus and his love for them. Manipulation of either the facts or of people is dishonest. *Spin* is wrong because its intent is to make something appear to be what it is not. Spreading false rumors about others is sin. But it is just as wrong to denigrate the reputations of others with innuendo. Withholding information from someone who has a right to know destroys trust. It is wrong to knowingly do so, but so is misleading people into believing something you know to be untrue. Cheating on taxes or while taking tests is not only unethical, it is immoral. For Christians, truth must be understood as an *uncompromisable* core value. When it comes to matters of truth and trust, we have an obligation to hold one another to a high standard of Christian integrity.

The apostle Paul wrote:

> It was he who gave some to be apostles, some to be prophets, some to be evangelists, and some to be pastors and teachers, to prepare God's people for works of service, so that the body of Christ may be built up until we all reach unity in the faith and in the knowledge of the Son of God and become mature, attaining to the whole measure of the fullness of Christ.

Then we will no longer be infants, tossed back and forth by the waves, and blown here and there by every wind of teaching and by the cunning and craftiness of men in their deceitful scheming. Instead, speaking the truth in love, we will in all things grow up into him who is the Head, that is, Christ. From him the whole body, joined and held together by every supporting ligament, grows and builds itself up in love, as each part does its work. (Ephesians 4:11-16)

Mistrust ignites more conflict than any other cause.

The Communication Factor

Stan Moralis and his wife, Emily, decided to send their children to Peace Lutheran School. This was not an easy decision. Both Stan and Emily are products of public education. And Emily teaches English at Mount Powell's public high school. The high cost of parochial education has made them both wonder if the money annually spent for the operation of the school and the child care center could be used in a better way.

While they have questions about the value of Peace Lutheran operating a parochial school, Stan and Emily have grown close to several of the teachers on the school's faculty, especially Steve and Jill Spiriak. Steve is the school's principal. Jill administers the child care.

Emily and Jill have made a point of having lunch together the first Tuesday of every month. They enjoy each other's company and value their friendship. They come from similar backgrounds, have the same likes and dislikes, see life from the same perspective, and lean on each other for encouragement and support. Imagine, then, how the Spiriaks felt when they heard that Stan Moralis had presented a plan to the Church Council to close the child care center and reduce the school staff by two teachers over the next two years.

Of course, that's not exactly what happened. To begin, Stan had not submitted a proposal. He had merely raised a question about how the school fit into the congregation's long-term future ministry plan. The conversation with the Church Council was meant to be confidential. The issues were discussed in good faith and with the congregation's best interests at heart. But somehow the conversation became public information and grist for the rumor mill. As the story spread, people embellished the facts. Soon Stan found himself carrying around the label of being *against Christian education.*

Communication plays a major role in conflict, both during the gathering storm and in the strategic approaches to finding resolution and restoring peace. Thankfully, the Bible has much to say about godly communication. Clearly, Scripture's primary message is that life eternal is ours through faith in Christ Jesus. But, in love, our heavenly Father has also established some valuable principles that govern communication and interaction among Christians. Conflict erects a stumbling block that interferes with the communication of God's primary message. God wants to help us avoid conflict. And when conflicts flare up (and they will), he wants us to have the communication tools needed to intervene so that the gospel can continue to flourish and accomplish its saving work unabated.

Intimacy Issues

Jill Spiriak was not responsible for starting the rumors that made Stan Moralis appear disloyal. But she did listen. Worse, she believed what she heard without making any attempt to verify the facts with Stan. As a result, she intentionally began to avoid Emily. She even stopped going to lunch with her friend on the first Tuesday of each month, claiming she was busy with family matters. Jill could not get past the feeling that she and Steve were being betrayed by Stan. Bitterness and resentment festered in her heart.

Relational breakdown occurs when one person, rightly or wrongly, comes to the conclusion that a dearly loved individual no longer shares the same feelings in return. Imagine the pain that accompanies such a revelation! Often the human response to this kind of news is, *"Then I will treat you in the same unloving way."*

Boundary Marking

The called staff at Peace Lutheran School and the workers at the child care center tried to rally. Steve made every effort to hold his faculty together. The teachers on his staff tried to remain positive. But it wasn't long before the threat to downsize began to take its toll.

Steve didn't want to believe these rumors. He was more inclined to blame Pastor Teschendorf for the arguing and hard feelings that were spreading throughout the congregation. Convinced that Pastor Teschendorf was pulling the strings, Steve began to publicly voice his doubt in Tim Teschendorf's commitment to the school and child care ministries. Pastor Teschendorf took this as a challenge to his authority.

Each teacher now began to wonder about his or her future at Peace Lutheran School. Faculty meetings became ordeals as individuals fought for shares of the school turf. Job security replaced humble service. Every-man-for-himself individualism replaced team attitudes.

Tensions also increased between the child care people and the school faculty. They soon stopped working together. Things got so bad that Steve and Jill were at times unable to discuss their situation without getting in each other's faces.

Turf battles and boundary issues can also cause bitter personal conflicts. Whenever Christians find themselves contending with coworkers for control over a definable area of the work, sin is much nearer than one may think.

Authority Issues and Competition for Control

For Pastor Teschendorf, the growing divisions at Peace Lutheran Church were very painful. During the past 17 years, Tim Teschendorf's last conscious thoughts before going to sleep were for the people of his congregation, whom he loved dearly. And his members loved him. But Tim's approach to leading was more along the lines of driving his flock: exerting strategic pressure in the right places, manipulating people, and maintaining control. As the congregation's spiritual leader, Tim saw himself as the final authority. And he jealously guarded that authority by making sure that he had his hand in virtually every decision. His underlying objective at most of the meetings he attended (and he attended them all) was to squelch criticism aimed at himself.

Those critical voices had lately been growing more intense. The budget shortfall raised new questions about the pastor's role. Some of his critics hinted that Tim might not be doing his job of bringing in new members. The criticism made Tim even more insecure.

Members of the school faculty and the people who worked in the child care facility wondered if Pastor Teschendorf still supported them. Sometimes it seemed as though the only thing he was interested in was protecting his own ministry turf.

The truth is that Tim Teschendorf was tired—tired of the endless meetings. He was also tired of the counseling sessions—patching up sick marriages and repairing twisted lives. He cried when Burt and Mary Ellen Grovner told him they were headed for a divorce and were no longer going to be coming in for his marriage counseling. Burt and Mary Ellen had met in Tim's first adult confirmation class at Peace. He had officiated at their wedding. This news broke his heart. Remarkably, over the years of counseling, Pastor Tim had tried hard to get them both to see that a marriage works much better when a husband and wife are not in competition for control. At the same time, Tim himself was not able to see that he was competing for control, sometimes with Steve Spiriak and the school faculty, sometimes with Jill. And sometimes he used the authority of his office to leverage control over decisions that needed to be made by the Church Council or the Spiritual Growth Committee.

Wars Unchosen

The case study here is far from complete. We've met only 9 of the 450 members of the Peace family. It lacks details about *what* was said, *to whom* it was said, and *how* it was said. Such details would be important if we were being asked to make a judgment about the moral grounds any one of these people may have for going to war with a fellow Christian. Our purpose here is to examine the generic causes for conflict, which are *(1) differences of opinion, (2) mistrust, (3) misunderstandings, (4) intimacy issues, (5) boundary marking, (6) issues regarding authority, and (7) competition for control.*

Each member involved in these disputes has a unique take on life at Peace Lutheran Church. Many others will eventually be drawn into the conflict. One thing is for sure: the conflicts at Peace are a tangled mess. Whatever the causes, the impacts will, without a doubt, shape the congregation's future.

The case study hints that some behaviors at Peace were mean-spirited. Does that necessarily imply violence? Hardly. It's more likely that the bitterest campaigns in this particular war will be fought with unkind words and icy stares. But it is still conflict. The expression *cold war* better suits the situation at Peace. In fact, most of the wars between individuals are of the *cold war* ilk. Cold wars consist more of lingering resentment, long-held grudges, and kindnesses withheld. They are a feeble attempt at walking the thin line (if there is such a thin line) between subtle expressions of lovelessness and hostile behaviors. Nevertheless, cold wars threaten to destroy the peace of our homes, schools, churches, and personal lives.

If we were to ask any of the people engaged in the conflict brewing at Peace Lutheran Church, they would probably say they had no choice; this war chose them.

While there are a few situations in which we have very little choice about going to war, most of the time that is simply not true. As a rule, conflict is a conscious choice, even if we arrive at a final decision in imperceptible, incremental steps.

One final observation before we move on. If asked, a few of the people engaged in this conflict would be honest enough to admit that they have, knowingly or intentionally, hurt someone who represents the opposition. This too is common. In the heat of battle, we are able to rationalize sinful behaviors that we would otherwise condemn.

For Thought and Discussion

- Which of the seven typical causes for conflict have reared their ugly heads in your life?

- Which one of the personal conflicts at Peace Lutheran Church seems to represent the most serious threat? Give a reason for your answer.

- Why do people generally tend to believe that conflict is thrust on them?

The Need to Justify

In Eden, before sin changed everything, Adam and Eve knew only one heart condition. Their hearts were always and only at peace with the Creator. They also were at peace with his creation, and with each other. In absolute terms, everything was right in those relationships. God provided for their every need. They lacked nothing and desired nothing more than to be in their Creator's favor and to share the joy of being in his presence and in each other's company.

Then they fell into the abyss of sin, and we suddenly see a new human need emerge. For the first time, Adam and Eve struggled to justify their behavior.[21] Something was telling them they must explain themselves and account for the choices they had made. First they hid. When that failed, Adam deferred to his nakedness as an excuse for hiding. Finally, they took turns playing *the blame game.* Adam blamed the woman. Eve claimed the serpent was her downfall. Their defense was hollow, feeble, and contrived. But their defense was also significant. Justifying disobedience would become a hallmark of every succeeding generation. All of humanity is now hardwired with the same moral circuitry for blaming others.[22]

We are accountable—to God, and to one another. A conscience, distorted by sin and quickened in the fall, still demands that we justify the immoral things we say and do. But making wrong behaviors right again is far beyond a sinner's reach.

A heart at war always faces a great risk. The odds that we will despise the enemy, hate him, curse him, lie about him, and seek to destroy him are exceedingly high. One best-selling secular book about conflict says, "When I am seeing others crookedly, what I need in that moment is justification, and I'll get it any way I can."[23] Even when the choice to engage is honorable and just, the engagement itself tends to lead us to embrace actions and behaviors that are not. The same source adds, "The more sure I am that I have been mistreated, the more likely I am to miss ways that I have mistreated others myself. My need for justification obscures the truth."

Not so for a heart that is at peace.

To understand how this works, we need to take a closer look at the word *justify*. Picture a bricklayer, busily constructing a wall. A tautly stretched string marks a straight line for the bricklayer to follow. If his line of bricks does not match the line established by the string, he must find a way to *justify* it—to make it right again.

But what if the bricklayer is blind? Then it will be impossible for him to change a crooked wall back into a straight one.

The human inclination to fix the crooked line of sin by ourselves is a powerful internal influence, even when the goal is not at all realistic. Our view of the life we need to justify is blinded by sin. Left to our own efforts, that life is doomed to remaining crooked. But that doesn't stop us from trying.

When our hearts are at war, we are like the bricklayer. We instinctively look for ways to make our wrongs appear to be right—to *justify* our words and actions. In fact, we can't stand living with ourselves until we can find ways to validate our behaviors.

For *sinners*—people for whom the truth is always a relative matter—there are a number of strategies that seem to suit our purposes. However, they really don't justify anything. These strategies only leave the appearance of being justified. But for some of us that may be enough to satisfy the insatiable hunger.

One simple response is to pretend that the walls of our lives are perfectly straight, even when we know they are not. Or we could ignore the fact of God and try to believe that he doesn't exist. Without God, it would only be necessary to pull the wool over the eyes of our neighbors, something most of us have been doing since long before the age of puberty.

Of course, there is a God; and he is very savvy about what goes on in our pretend lives. He does not buy the act. God knows a crooked line when he sees one.

Without God, it would only be necessary to pull the wool over the eyes of our neighbors, something most of us have been doing since the age of puberty.

If eliminating God seems a little extreme, maybe we can convince ourselves (and others) that he is no longer relevant or that he doesn't really mean what he says. These strategies work if one can somehow ignore the eternal consequences of violating the boundaries that a loving God has set for us and our neighbors.[24] God fences us off from many dangers and pitfalls by placing the whole human race under the same laws.[25] These are reasonable laws. They are just. Without them, a civil society could not last a day.

I may be able to justify my at-war words and actions by acting as if I am above the law. Then I am not required to answer for the bad choices I make. In the real world, even kings and princes are consigned to living under God's law, though they may not always like it.

Have you ever tried using some of these strategies? They may work when we are trying to justify our actions to other people. They never work with God.

While the need to be justified is true of every crooked behavior, it is especially true for those behaviors that occur when relationships turn sour.[26]

How We View Others

Both ways of being—at peace and at war—cast broad shadows on the way we view others. When I relate to another individual with a heart that is at peace, I see that person in a way similar to the way I see myself. I see him or her as a human being who has hopes, needs, cares, and dreams, just as I have. It takes a heart at peace to "do to others what you would have them do to you" (Matthew 7:12).

But when I relate to others with a heart that is inclined toward war, I see them as obstacles that stand in the way of my success. I see them as vehicles to be used and abused in order to achieve my own ends. When I approach a relationship with a heart at peace, I can see a potential partner in the other person, someone who is able to bring me added blessings. With a heart at war, I can only see someone who is irrelevant to the things that are important to me.

With a heart at war, I am inclined to view my enemy as an object. I may even imagine that my enemy is the devil incarnate. This explains why a Christian engaged in conflict may actually ask God to damn a fellow human being to hell.

When I view an enemy with a heart that is at peace, I can still see him or her as a human being. I can respect the person's rights, name, reputation, life.

A Favorite Game

One of the most sinister strategies for justifying wrongful behaviors is a mental game that is prompted by the question, *Who's on top?* The game board resembles a ladder. Every position on this ladderlike structure is relative to every other position. You can rise above another player's position, or you can find yourself on a lower rung.

Of course, this is not really a game at all; it is a way of life—a mind-set that sinful humankind has devised in order to view others in a way that allows us to justify behaviors that are neither peaceful nor loving. But here's the irony: The object of the game is not so much about striving for and attaining the ladder's summit. The real object of the game is to justify the horrible things you did to judge and punish your opponents.

The players in my game of Who's on Top? are there because I have relationships with them. You have your own game going, with a full complement of relationships that can at any time be made active or inactive according to the condition of your own heart. We're at war with those we have activated. The rest are in a holding pattern. We will remain temporarily at peace with those in the holding tank until a time when being at war with them suits our own purposes. Some of my relationships will spend more active time on the game board than others. When they are active, I will despise them. And I will work very hard to judge them and punish them. That is how the game is played.

One other thing about this game: No matter where each player is positioned on the ladderlike structure, the potential is always there to find an advantage. If I can see myself as being better off than someone with whom I am at war, I will think of that person as insignificant, subhuman, and irrelevant. Because I am in a superior position, I will generally see myself as wise, right, and honest while my inferior appears foolish, wrong, and dishonest. In my superior position, I can also justify my impatience, disdain, and indifference toward my inferior. In short, I can treat that person as an object.

If, on the other hand, my position is inferior to my enemy's, I can still rationalize my hostile behaviors. After all, such an enemy has probably gained higher rank and status by taking everything he or she has *from me.* And there's little doubt that this was done in a dishonorable or dishonest manner. That explains why he or she is wealthier, more fortunate, more blessed than I am. From an inferior position, I will be inclined to view my enemy as privileged or advantaged. This gives rise to my feelings of jealousy, bitterness, helplessness, even depression. But it also provides the kind of justification I need to treat that individual as subhuman.

To play this game, you and I must be prepared to judge others relative to their social status, economic position, moral character, intellectual acuity, political ranking, communal standing, skill level, level of education, and a host of other criteria. Small wonder this *game* spawns cultural bias, racial bigotry, ethnic prejudice, gender chauvinism, intolerance, and all the other kinds of favoritism that falsely justify cruel and inhuman conduct!

The apostle James wrote with force and clarity about such games: "My brothers, as believers in our glorious Lord Jesus Christ, don't show favoritism. . . . If you really keep the royal law found in Scripture, 'Love your neighbor as yourself,' you are doing right. But if you show favoritism, you sin and are convicted by the law as lawbreakers. For whoever keeps the whole law and yet stumbles at just one point is guilty of breaking all of it" (2:1,8-10).

James later amplified his remarks, writing, "If you harbor bitter envy or selfish ambition in your hearts, do not boast about it or deny the truth. Such 'wisdom' does not come down from heaven but is earthly, unspiritual, of the devil. For where you have envy and selfish ambition, there you find disorder and every evil practice. But the wisdom that comes from heaven is first of all pure; then peace-loving, considerate, submissive, full of mercy and good fruit, impartial and sincere" (3:14-17).

For Thought and Discussion

- List some of the risks that are in play when we make the choice to be at war.
- Why does prejudice so often lead to conflict? How does personal prejudice obstruct, hinder, or undermine the gospel's spread?
- Describe some *games* you play when you are at war with others.

High Ground, Slippery Slopes, and Bottomlands

T. S. Eliot wrote, "Humankind cannot bear very much reality." How true. When conflict threatens to destroy us, we do our best to find a solution. But we do not always deal with our conflicts in the same way or employ the same strategies for untangling our hate-filled messes. In his book *The Peacemaker*, author Ken Sande depicts a range of 12 conflict-resolution strategies as a "slippery slope." (See Illustration 1.)[27] This panoramic view shows that at least half of our conflict-resolution strategies are actually negative and destructive.

On the downside of the left slope lie three strategies: *suicide, flight,* and *denial.* Sande describes these as *escape strategies,* calling them *peace fakers* because they are imposters. They merely pretend to offer resolution.

Suicide is both self-directed and self-destructive. The conflicts within a person who is about to take his or her own life is generally more intense than any external conflicts. Suicide rightly deserves to be classified as a *peace faker.* With its only purpose being to avoid pain, suicide is obviously a nonstarter.

At the bottom of the slope on the right lie three attack strategies: *murder, assault,* and *litigation.*[28] Sande calls these *peace breakers* because they either intensify an existing conflict or produce a new one. These three strategies on the far end of the right slope are all *others-directed* actions. The purpose for each of them is to do maximum damage to an enemy.[29]

Under some circumstances, *flight* and *litigation* can effectively lead to positive outcomes. In the main, however, even those two strategies are generally weak for resolving serious conflict. The other four just mentioned are unacceptable.

Halfway up the slope on the left side of the summit lie two exciting strategies that have huge potential for leading us to peace—*overlooking* and *calling someone to account for moral wrong*.

Overlooking appears passive, though the choice is certainly intentional. Overlooking is more of a *conflict-*

OUR STRATEGIES FOR RESOLVING CONFLICT

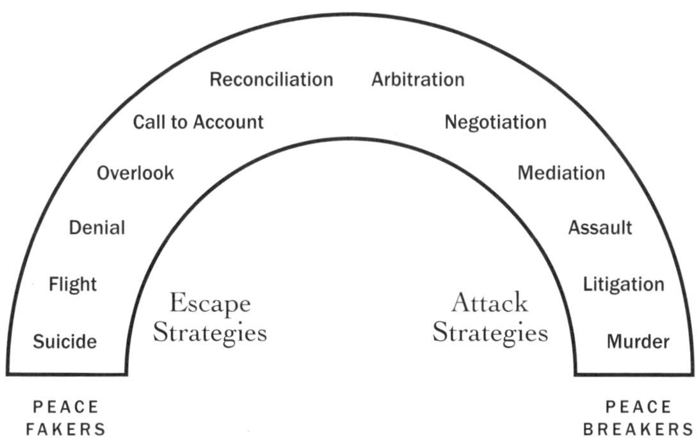

Adapted from "The Slippery Slope of Conflict."
© Peacemaker® Ministries. Used by permission. www.Peacemaker.net

management strategy. In contrast to *denial,* which is almost always an emotion-based strategy, overlooking an offense can often have a sound rationale behind the choice. The aim usually is to defuse conflict before it can develop. But there is a caveat that comes with overlooking. In conflict, overlooking can require an enormous amount of patience. Besides, looking the other way can clearly be an inappropriate response under certain circumstances. When, for example, an abused individual lacks the resources to mount a defense (a child being bullied or a mentally handicapped person being harassed), caregivers need to pursue a less passive course than overlooking the offense.

Calling someone to account for immoral behavior is an active, aggressive strategy that takes the form of an indictment, which demands reasonable evidence to support its claim.

Calling someone to account for sinful behavior can be motivated by sincere Christian love and concern. Its purpose, then, is to lead a sinner to repentance, reconciliation, healing, and restoration to Christ's body of believers. In the church militant, this strategy is often referred to as *church discipline.* Under the heading of *the Office of the Keys,* Luther couples *calling someone to account for sin* with *reconciliation.* We will be discussing both of these strategies in greater detail in Part Two of this book. The three formal strategies (*arbitration, negotiation,* and *mediation*) that lie near the hill's summit on the right side of the illustration will also be discussed in later chapters as intervention strategies.

Sande's illustration helps us see how failing to seek the high ground will eventually degenerate into a deadly slide down one of the slopes. James explored this inevitability when he wrote, "Each one is tempted when, by his own evil desire, he is dragged away and enticed. Then, after desire has conceived, it gives birth to sin; and sin, when it is full-grown, gives birth to death" (1:14,15).

Daring to Deny

Jesus had gone to the temple early to teach. He was sketching in the sand to illustrate a point when a handful of Jewish leaders rudely interrupted. With a woman in tow, they angrily waved rocks picked up from the street. The woman had been caught in the act of adultery. According to the Torah, her crime was a felony, punishable by stoning. However, the venue for her trial was highly unusual. This type of business was normally conducted behind closed doors, not in the street. The temple leaders seemed more interested in putting Jesus on public trial. They wanted to expose him as a radical. The young rabbi had been challenging their theological integrity. Perhaps they could bait him into saying something treasonous or make him appear to condone promiscuity. "How would you judge this whore?" one of them asked.

Jesus ignored them. He had no jurisdiction in the matter.

Not used to being ignored, the religious leaders persisted, "What do you say, rabbi?"

Finally, Jesus stopped teaching and stood to face them. "If any one of you is without sin," he said quietly, "let him be the first to throw a stone at her" (John 8:7). Then he went back to the lesson.

"Without sin"? Jesus knew about their indiscretions.[30] *One by one they dropped their stones . . . and the indictment. They were afraid he would expose them. None was willing to risk that.*

One of the most difficult things you or I will ever face in life is admitting our own sins. That is especially true if

One of the most difficult things we can ever face in life is admitting our own sins.

our transgressions have been defined in specific terms. Admitting that we have hated another person is a particularly hard thing to do. The words *I'm sorry* are the two most difficult words to say in any language.

What if people really knew what you and I are capable of—our plans for revenge; our hatred and jealousies; our greed, intolerance, arrogance; our profane longings and lustful desires; . . . our self-idolatry? We shudder at the thought. Most of us spend a lifetime devising ways to keep such things out of sight. Social stigma is a powerful influence. But exposure in the court of God's holy justice is more profound.[31] The eternal future of those temple leaders might have been different had they only heeded Jesus' words and repented.

When we are paralyzed with fear, it's not hard to pretend that everything is just fine, even when it isn't. Sometimes we work so hard at secreting the darkness hidden in our hearts that we are able to convince ourselves of the lie. This is called *denial.*

Denial is conflict driven into the nethermost places of the heart. When there, an individual mistakenly believes he or she will not have to acknowledge it.

Like the decision to live with a heart that is at war, denial is a choice. One writer says it "involves active avoidance . . . a deliberate effort to refrain from even noticing [that something is wrong]. . . . It usually involves refusing to acknowledge the presence of things that beg for attention."[32]

Often the motivation for denial is fear. But the fear may not always be a response to our own pain. Sometimes we avoid seeing the sins of a loved one. This can become an ongoing pretense, like someone pretending not to notice the disfiguring scars on the face of the burn victim to whom he has just been introduced. Out of compassion we do our best to avoid looking directly at the disturbing sight.

But pretending not to notice can also make a relationship awkward and uncomfortable. While deception is not the intent, we go out of our way not to see something that is painfully obvious. Unless the pretense itself is acknowledged, any hope for a meaningful relationship will continue to be compromised.

When sin is part of the equation, denial is a silent faith killer. Here Satan is especially crafty, providing a tempting smorgasbord of three possible truths to deny. All three are spiritually lethal. The first option Satan places before us is to deny the truth of sin (ours or that of someone else who is dear to us).[33] Alternately, he dangles the choice of denying Jesus' power and authority to forgive sin.[34] If these ploys don't work, he tries to get us to deny the *new self*—that *new man* rooted in Christ's love. The devil knows that the *new man* wants to do the right thing. He also knows that the choice to deny the *new-man* inclination is a choice to go to war with God . . . again.[35]

The Pharisees' fundamental problem was that they were living in a perpetual state of denial. Denying their own sinfulness is what launched their conflict with Jesus in the first place. When he lovingly tried to intervene, their denial led them to reject him out of hand. They did their best not to acknowledge the *elephant in the room* that had crowded God out of their lives. Repentance was within reach, and with it forgiveness. Jesus gave them a perfect opportunity to do some serious soul-searching. Yet because they were in full denial, the father of lies had them right where he wanted them.

Emperors and Elephants

Someone once observed, "It only takes one person to produce speech, but it requires the cooperation of all to produce silence."[36] History has its share of corporate silences. The Holocaust, for example, will not be remembered so much for the extraordinary numbers of people murdered in gas chambers as it will be remembered for the silent conspiracy that permitted such an unthinkable thing to happen.

A metaphor for this phenomenon is the familiar parable of "The Emperor's New Clothes." In the Hans Christian Andersen version, con artists have convinced a vain and gullible emperor that they have invented a magical thread that can only be seen by folks who are not fools. The emperor falls for the swindle and orders a new suit woven from the magic thread. His royal subjects will thrill to see him attired in this remarkable new cloth, and the enchanting fabric will help him spot the fools in his court.

Naturally, at his first fitting the emperor recognizes that he is completely naked. But noticing and acknowledging are two very different matters. To avoid exposure as a fool, the emperor *oohs* and *aahs* at the make-believe garment. His courtiers also pretend not to notice anything unusual. Instead, they encourage him to wear the new duds in a royal procession scheduled for the next day.

The next day, when the emperor's entourage parades down the crowded avenue, his subjects enthusiastically applaud the rich colors and luxurious textures of his new ensemble. Of course, they've been told that only the brightest people in the land can see the exotic new fibers.

Then a boy, who has little understanding of the implications of what he is saying and no compunctions about exposing His Royal Highness, steps out of the crowd, shouting, "Look! The emperor isn't wearing any clothes!"

The story accurately describes a social phenomenon we are all familiar with. Entertaining as the tale is, real-world corporate denial can lead to devastating outcomes.

The *elephant-in-the-room syndrome* is an extension of personal denial. "Conspiracies of silence presuppose mutual denial."[37] They make a point of declaring that *we don't have a problem,* creating a block between the private act of noticing and the public act of acknowledging.[38]

Silent conspiracies function within a subculture that is systemically organized to nurture *no-go zones.* These zones are to be treated as though they don't exist. Communities (families, groups, congregations, etc.) leverage the power of a silent conspiracy whenever uncomfortable truths are hidden in plain sight. "By simply watching others ignore certain things, we learn to ignore them as well. ('. . . Seeing that nobody around her ever mentioned her father's drinking, Sarah likewise understood that it was something she was not supposed to notice.')"[39]

A conspiracy of silence, like other cultural beliefs, can be passed from generation to generation. Everyone is expected to comply. Those who don't are usually eyed with suspicion and treated as social deviants. "As such, [they] are the targets of various social sanctions."[40]

The lad who observed that the emperor was naked hadn't yet learned what he was supposed to acknowledge or not acknowledge. In real life, whistle-blowers pay a steep price for committing sins that threaten to expose the whole community.

On the landscape of the church, the close relationship between conflict and sin cannot be emphasized too much. But because we have (correctly) been taught to "put the best construction on everything,"[41] God's people are inclined to see conflict merely as two individuals with competing interests. Any mention of sin in connection with conflict is often met with overwhelming silence. No one close to the situation would ever see silence as a conspiracy. In fact, they have never really given much thought to the problem as being a *problem.*

The motivation for a conspiracy of silence is not necessarily mean-spirited, spiteful, or malicious. One of the great ironies of corporate conspiracy is that it is all about self-preservation and maintaining peace. A conspiracy of silence provides a kind of protective shell around information and communication. Protected by this shell, things can continue to function in a relatively normal manner for some time. But the shell also effectively eliminates any hope for reconciliation and healing.

Church subcultures can be very fragile. Talk about corporate sin has the ring of fighting words. To counter, we are willing to permit *the elephant* to live in our room as a trade-off for initiating a sequence of events that could spin wildly out of control. The known of a growing elephant is far less intimidating than the unknown of what could happen if we discuss the issue as an authentic problem. To put it another way, living with an elephant is seen as less painful than the pain connected with getting rid of the elephant. If the elephant is ever to be exposed (and removed), someone will need to blow the whistle.

Jeremiah blasted the Jewish leaders of his day for declaring, "'Peace, peace,' . . . when there is no peace."[42] The spiritual leaders had nurtured a climate in which the people whom they were called to lead were led to believe that all was well when, in fact, sin was running rampant. This elephant had been growing within the Jerusalem culture for several generations and was now endemic to Jewish faith life. The lie was literally leading God's people on the path to spiritual ruin. Some knew this was wrong, but they did nothing about it.

Abraham Lincoln is quoted as having said, "To sin by silence when they should protest makes cowards of men."[43] Denying that conflict exists is as dangerous as denying sin. An old saw bluntly asserts that *if you are not part of the solution, you are part of the problem.* When one's conscience says that speaking up is the only right thing to do, failing to speak is sin.

More About the Elephants Living in Our Homes

Family dysfunction often occurs when the agenda is to hide the shameful behavior of one family member. There is extreme pressure on everyone to maintain "a silence about things whose open discussion would threaten the group's solidarity, . . . to break the silence [would be] considered an attack against the group, a sort of treason."[44]

In such a family dynamic, it is virtually impossible to move forward, to grow in mutual love for one another, to serve one another, to learn from one another, to be completely honest with one another, to encourage and support one another.

When you have an elephant living at your house, conflict is not the immediate threat. Fear of being exposed is the engine that drives almost everything that happens. Everyone walks on eggshells. The pain of shame is internalized. Individuals become isolated. Honest communication suffers or becomes nonexistent. Trust grows fragile. Relationships deteriorate. Hope turns to hopelessness. Faith is placed in jeopardy. Resolution is seen as all but impossible.

Children will tell you that *elephants eat a lot. When they eat, they poop. They keep getting bigger. They break things. They're a lot of work. They are hard to hide. They don't leave room for anyone else in the room. And they're hard to control.* Kids may not always be savvy about denial, but they know their elephants. Reread the observations that children have made about elephants, and you will immediately understand why it is so necessary to remove the elephants of denial from a dysfunctional home environment.

Getting rid of an elephant is not easy. But with God's help it can be done. Here are ten suggestions to help a Christian family overcome the paralysis of corporate denial:

1. Pray alone. Then pray together.
2. Include God in your family conversations.
3. Invite open and honest comments.
4. Be prepared to accept your own flaws and shortcomings.
5. Rehearse what you will say.
6. Stay on topic.
7. Speak the truth in love.
8. Communicate at a rational level, remaining calm and unemotional.
9. Provide constructive solutions.
10. Extend the conversation.

An Urgent Matter

At the onset of the American Civil War, no one foresaw the tremendous cost of such a conflict, either in terms of lives lost or economic sacrifices made. The risks that accompany the choice of living with an at-war heart can be profound. Bad things happen in war—unexpected things. A conflagration can look very different before it is fought from the way the battlefield will look when the smoke finally clears. Casualties can far exceed projections. Political outcomes can be thoroughly unpredictable. Endgames are often elusive. There are plenty of good reasons for seeing conflict as an urgent matter and seeking a solution as a high priority.

God speaks about conflict in his Word as if it is an urgent matter. He wants his people to see peace as an important objective. Jesus used a word picture to drive this point home: "If you are offering your gift at the altar and there remember that your brother has something against you, leave your gift there in front of the altar. First go and be reconciled to your brother; then come and offer your gift" (Matthew 5:23,24). Can you sense the urgency? When conflict is looming, making an effort to reconcile takes precedence even over worship.

If anyone understands hatred, Jesus certainly does. He experienced it in the extreme. He knows pain too. Surely he is interested in the battle statistics of every human conflict. His work of curing the sick, healing the demon possessed, restoring sight to the blind, and raising the dead provides ample evidence of how deeply and compassionately he cares about our grief-stricken hearts. There should be no doubt about his loving concern for anyone languishing in the terror of real conflict, whether it is at the loss of a loved one who has made the ultimate sacrifice for his or her country or merely at the hurt feelings that come from a hateful comment.

But, for Jesus, the urgency is rooted in his desire to guard the hearts of those who get caught up in conflict. He knows how conflict can strip us of our humanity. He knows that when our hearts are at war, we will dwell on the injustices we have suffered in order to keep our hatred alive. He knows we need enemies to justify the evil plans we have for destroying them. He knows that our *old Adam* wants war more than it wants peace. He knows that the outward wars we engage in started because of inward wars that went unnoticed. He knows that an unresolved inner war is the very germ of human conflict.

As carriers, we are all wars just waiting to happen. And Jesus knows that the toll for engagement can be spiritually fatal. St. John wrote, "Anyone who claims to be in the light but hates his brother is still in the darkness. Whoever loves his brother lives in the light, and there is nothing in him to make him stumble. But whoever hates his brother is in the darkness and walks around in the darkness; he does not know where he is going, because the darkness has blinded him" (1 John 2:9-11).

Could the stakes be any higher?

For Thought and Discussion

- How is Sande's illustration helpful for our understanding of conflict resolution?

- Have you had personal experience with some of these responses to conflict?

- Is there an *elephant in the room* at your church, school, business, or in your family?

- Make a short list of reasons why we need to address personal conflict as an urgent matter. Which item on your list is the most compelling?

CHAPTER 6

On Earth Peace to Men

Heavy flakes of snow started falling sometime around noon. By mid-afternoon a blanket of white covered the ground. This would be the first white Christmas anyone in Mount Powell could remember. Every street corner, avenue, and side road looked as though it had been scrubbed clean to welcome the miracle child of Bethlehem. With its stately steeple and gorgeous stained-glass windows glowing from within, Peace Lutheran Church stood near the center of town with two snow-dusted wreaths hanging on the big oak doors, looking like a Hallmark greeting card.

Inside, folks craned their necks to catch sight of their children proudly walking two-by-two down the aisle to the front of the church—daughters and granddaughters dressed in festive greens, reds, and maroons; sons and grandsons all tidy and neat. Infectious smiles spanned their scrubbed faces and warmed the hearts of worshipers.

The congregation sang a robust version of "A Great and Mighty Wonder." The children chimed in for each refrain: *"Repeat the hymn again: 'To God on high be glory and peace on earth to men.'"*

Pastor Teschendorf led the procession. Steve Spiriak guided the older children into the pews to which they had been assigned during the practice earlier in the week. The two men had not spoken to each other in three weeks.

The Staff Meeting

Tim and Steve had last been together during a staff meeting in early December where the atmosphere had crackled with tension. Both the school staff and the child care staff tried to meet at least once a month with the pastor. Several of the faculty members had privately shared their concerns with Steve in the weeks leading up to the meeting. They felt Pastor Tim was manipulating the church's agenda in a way that would eventually lead to the closing of either the child care center or the school, or both. The staff meeting was their first opportunity to air these concerns. Some of them had asked if they could also attend the next meeting of the Christian Education Committee. They trusted Mark Eastman as the committee's chairman and believed the people serving on that board were working hard to stop the gathering momentum from destroying their congregation's educational programs. Some of the staff members blamed Pastor Teschendorf. They felt that he and Stan Moralis were the main proponents of the movement to close their programs down. The general feeling was that this was Tim Teschendorf's response to all the criticism he was getting for his ride-herd leadership style.

During the meeting Steve felt he was speaking for the others. He tried to control his voice but was visibly shaking as he spoke: "You say you support us, Pastor Teschendorf. But when the time comes for giving us the support we need, you put our school program down and undermine the work being done at the child care center. Worse, you don't respect our right to have a voice in this mess. You say that we're not called here to lead—that we have no say. But you have no problem setting the agenda for every program in the church, even though you are also the congregation's called servant. We care about this congregation. We care about the ministry that our school and child care programs represent. We have a right to speak. And you have no right to silence us."

Tim Teschendorf got red as the principal spoke. Several times during the meeting he addressed Steve as "*Mister* Spiriak," spitting out the *mister* to show his disdain. "Your problem, Mister Spiriak, is that you are a territorial animal. You're intentionally stirring up the members in order to drive a wedge between supporters of the school and the anti-school people. If this '*mess,*' as you called it, were left to you, it would only get worse. Eventually the whole parish would come to ruin just to serve your personal interests in running that school. That won't go around here. I won't allow it."

The pastor's words were still echoing in Steve's ears as he listened to a reading of the Christmas gospel from the first chapter of John. He had not had a decent night's sleep since that awful meeting. Even though he was just trying to be honest, Steve wished he had not been so blunt in reacting to Pastor Teschendorf's stinging accusation. "Pastor," he had said, "the congregation couldn't be any more divided than it is right now. And it's not because of me or our education program. It's divided over you and the way you lead."

The meeting had made one thing clear: Steve Spiriak and Tim Teschendorf were not on the same page. The gospel partnership that the apostle Paul had once written about to the Christians at Philippi was broken at Peace Church, or at the very least badly damaged.[45] The joy of working together, of supporting one another's ministry, of being grateful for the blessings of having a common faith with a common purpose had all but vanished. Neither side was going to back down. Positions were becoming passionate, and viewpoints, entrenched. Exhausted, Steve went through the motions and tried to concentrate on the children's presentation of the Christmas story.

Feeling the Pain

The joy of Christmas had also been dampened for Emily Moralis. She was saddened by the breach in her relationship with Jill Spiriak. Emily was now certain that she had lost a best friend and her closest confidante, probably forever. That night, before the service, Jill had made every effort to ignore her. When Emily had made an effort to seek Jill out to greet her, Jill had turned the other way to avoid her. Here it was Christmas Eve and they had not spoken to each other. It was intentional!

Emily wondered if Jill was hurting as badly as she was. *If that's the way Jill wants our relationship to go,* reasoned Emily, *I'm not going to go out of my way to try to change her mind.*

Each class took a turn at narrating a portion of the story, starting with the Old Testament prophecies about the Savior's coming. The third grade children spoke in chorus, loudly and in perfect unison. They recounted the prophetic words of Isaiah 9:6, foretelling the coming Messiah's action-names: "For to us a child is born, to us a son is given, and the government will be on his shoulders. And he will be called Wonderful Counselor, Mighty God, Everlasting Father, Prince of Peace."

As Mark Eastman sat and listened to his daughter's class recount the prophet's words, he wondered why he felt such inner turmoil. Jesus had come to bring the peace of God's full and free forgiveness to all people.

Why, then, was this year's celebration of the Christmas miracle so clouded with sadness and anxiety? As he studied the faces of the people sitting around him, he knew he wasn't the only one deeply troubled by what was going on. He also knew that with every passing day, more folks would become engaged in what was still just a quiet little war. He wondered how long it would be before the wheels would come off altogether. In his mind the conflict needed to be resolved now, before it would be too late and the congregation suffered more losses.

Then the whole assembly of children sang Tim Teschendorf's favorite Christmas hymn. It laid out the gospel so beautifully with the words "unasked, unforced, unearned" to describe the unconditional love that drove God to come to earth on that first Christmas.[46] Nothing was more precious than God's grace: a love so boundless that God himself would come to live as a man among sinners and die, even for those who hated him.

Tim struggled to regain his focus for preaching the brief homily. It was based on verse 14 in Luke chapter 2—the words sung by angels over the Bethlehem hills: "Glory to God in the highest, and *on earth peace to men* on whom his favor rests." What a sweet song those blessed shepherds heard!

But Tim found it hard to concentrate. Other matters intruded. This Christmas had undoubtedly been the most difficult in his career. Tim wished he did not feel the way he did about some of the congregation's leaders—in particular, those who were constantly challenging his pastoral authority. He wanted to believe they meant well. But they questioned every move he made. A generation ago no one would have dared to say some of the things these people were saying about their pastor. How could a man be at peace when he was under such intense scrutiny?

Tim's confidence had been shaken. Sometime around Thanksgiving he had opened his heart to Stan Moralis, the chairman of the congregation: "We've got to put a stop to this rebellious attitude," he told Stan. "I'm afraid we're going to have to deal with Mark Eastman and Steve Spiriak."

Stan seemed to be on board. He had even said, "Very few people in the congregation trust Mark Eastman." But Tim had caught the devilish look in Stan's eyes when he said this.

The children's portion of the program ended. It was time for Tim Teschendorf to preach the sermon he had prepared. As he looked out over the assembly, he saw the dear people of his congregation. How he loved them! How he wanted the bickering to stop! But he had no idea of where to begin. His own leadership had eroded, compromised by his strong opinions and blunt tone. He wondered when he had lost his edge and why. As a student at the seminary many years earlier, Tim Teschendorf had always thought of himself as a strong leader, even among his peers. Now some of his strongest supporters had stopped listening to him. The number of disaffected members had grown. It made him wonder, *How can a pastor lead such stubborn people?* Still, he was sure he was pursuing the right course. God had called him to lead, and he was doing the best he could under difficult circumstances. He began, "My dear Christian friends, . . ."

Ned Constantino was also hurting. He had seen the problem between Stan Moralis and Mark Eastman developing more than a year ago when Stan had publicly filed a lawsuit against his former business partner. Ned had always tried to remain friendly to both men. At the same time, he was convinced that the Spiritual Growth Committee needed to take an active role in bringing these two men together to help them resolve the animosity between them. Tonight Stan had come to offer a warm Christmas greeting to Ned and his wife. They talked small talk for a while. Then Stan let it slip that he thought the time had come to deal with Mark Eastman and the Christian Education Committee (CEC), adding, "The pastor's already on board with the idea of making some changes."

It was a hard conversation for Ned to digest. *What had Stan meant? Mark and the other CEC members had a right to speak their minds.* To his knowledge, Mark had done nothing to deserve such treatment—not from Stan Moralis or anyone else. Ned wondered if Pastor Teschendorf could really be on board with such an idea.

In Conflict . . . and Alone

Burt Grovner sat passively in the very last pew of the church. He was alone. Mary Ellen had refused to go with him. The fight they had that afternoon was more like an all-out war. They hated each other; that much was clear. And no matter how much Pastor Teschendorf tried to counsel them to remain together, their hatred for each other would never be overcome. Burt was certain of that. Today's fight was just another *nail in the coffin* of their dead marriage. They couldn't even be civil to each other on Christmas Eve. Tonight Burt had come to church, hoping to find some peace of mind. He heard everything that the children said—the blessed Christmas story, spoken and sung from their little hearts of faith. He tried to absorb Pastor Teschendorf's message about peace on earth. Nothing was registering. In his world there seemed to be fighting in every direction he turned. The peace he sought seemed so distant and out of reach. All he could feel was the mind-numbing rage he felt for Mary Ellen. He knew it was wrong; he just couldn't help himself. She had made their lives together a living hell.

Pastor Teschendorf had once tried to convince Burt that being bitter and hating someone is a choice we make. Burt had not agreed or disagreed. There were times when he actually thought of his wife as the devil incarnate. He had even confessed having this notion to the pastor. Pastor Teschendorf's response had been, "Difficult choices are still choices, and difficult people are still people who are washed clean in the blood of God's Lamb. It is always within our power to see them in that way."

For a while Burt had tried to see Mary Ellen *in that way*—as a sinner washed clean in Jesus' blood. But he knew her too well; he understood the evil things she was capable of saying and doing. The fighting had continued until any hope for reconciliation had disappeared. Now here he was on Christmas Eve, filled with disappointment and anger—much of it self-directed. He had played a significant role in destroying their marriage. The guilt was eating him up. But Mary Ellen had to accept her share of the blame. And that would never happen.

Halfway through the service Burt got up and left to find peace somewhere else.

For Thought and Discussion

- Why is it difficult for Christians who have never experienced the kinds of personal conflicts described in this chapter to relate to them?

- Who seems to be in the greatest jeopardy at Peace Lutheran Church? Explain.

- Why do you think the individuals at Peace Lutheran Church are having a difficult time making the connection between the Christmas gospel's comforting message and the conflicts in which they are engaged?

CHAPTER 7

The Gathering Storm

After the holidays, the perfect storm of conflict at Peace Lutheran Church quietly gained momentum. A few members recognized the impending threat. For most, however, the gathering storm clouds were barely on the radar. If they knew about the rifts at all, they were seen as minor disturbances. Like a common cold, things would return to normal when each problem had run its course.

Jill Spiriak and Emily Moralis knew it was more than an empty threat. This was a test. And, in her own way, each had failed. How carelessly they had allowed their friendship to slip away! What a shameful waste! The prospect of ever repairing it seemed remote, maybe even impossible. Too much heartache had already been inflicted. Too much injury and pain had been suffered for either woman to be convinced that their shattered friendship might ever be salvaged.

Then, in late February, during one of the worst snowstorms anyone could remember, God intervened, sending Tim Teschendorf to the hospital with severe chest pain.

According to the cardiologist, the infarction was serious. Several blockages needed immediate attention. Surgery was scheduled for the next day. Tim would have to stay in the hospital for a few days. After that, he was supposed to rest for several weeks. In the doctor's words,

"Stay away from the daily grind at the office. Get someone to preach for the next three Sundays. And no evening meetings."

It was not the kind of news Tim wanted to hear. He called his secretary from his hospital bed and instructed her to cancel the church council meeting scheduled for that night.

The snowstorm had been growing in intensity all afternoon. None of the men who received the e-mail had time to read it. When they arrived at church, the council members were surprised to hear that their pastor was in the hospital and the meeting had been cancelled.

The news frustrated Ned Constantino more than the others. He had driven a long way in the raging blizzard. Furthermore, he doubted that Pastor Teschendorf had the authority to cancel the meeting. "We've got plenty of things to discuss that wouldn't require our pastor's input," said Ned.

"That's crazy," barked Stan. "How can we meet without him?"

Ned tried to galvanize the group with some humor. "Come on, Stan, we don't want to go back out into that weather. In an hour or two, it'll blow itself out. In the meanwhile, we can talk about a few things that need attention."

"Like what?" shot back Stan. He surveyed the room, trying to decide if he had enough support in the event that the meeting turned contentious.

More council members shuffled in and sat down at the conference table. Burt Grovner asked for an agenda.

As the president of the congregation and chairman of the church council, Stan was in the habit of preparing a single-page agenda, which Pastor Teschendorf would approve. But this evening Stan had needed to snow blow his driveway so that he could get to the meeting. He had run out of time for creating the new agenda.

Ned had been praying for such an opportunity. "Off the record," he began, "I'd like to ask a question: Why can't we seem to get along with one another in this church?"

The room became silent. It was not the direction Stan wanted things to take. Trying to ignore Ned's question, Stan growled, "Okay, you guys want to talk; let's start with the school. And let me just say one thing to set the record straight: We have trouble getting along here because there's an elephant in the room. We have to make some hard choices to get rid of it. Over the last ten years, our school enrollment has seen a decline of almost 25 percent. We can't keep going down that path. It's not fiscally sound . . . or good stewardship!"

The opening give-and-take between Stan and Ned caught Mark Eastman off guard. The meetings normally began with a brief devotion. No one had volunteered tonight. Mark tried to catch up: "Do you really think closing the school will change the dynamic here, Stan? We've got a lot of other things to address before that will make a difference."

Outside, the wind howled in the dark night, and beads of ice pelted the windows.

Ned felt immediately drawn to Mark's argument: "Stan, you know I don't always agree with Mark. But he's right about one thing: We do have other issues here at Peace. Look at our statistics. Worship attendance is abysmal. Communion attendance continues to slide. Participation in Bible study is way off. When's the last time we had an adult confirmation? We're not the strong, vibrant church we were a generation ago. We're a dying congregation. The elephant we're all afraid to talk about isn't the school or the child care center; it's the spiritual health of our members that we keep avoiding."

The conversation resonated with Steve Spiriak. He was tired of watching the school's enrollment slide year after year. As principal, that was his burden. However, Steve still blamed Pastor Teschendorf for failing to support the other called coworkers on the staff. Yet the last thing he wanted was to appear disloyal. "We have trouble looking into the mirror to honestly evaluate our work here," he said. "We're so focused on our financial problems that we've forgotten what the real mission is. We're afraid to change what we're doing. If anything is going to improve, we're going to have to deal first with our fears and our denial."

"Denial," shouted Stan. "What are we denying? Given our circumstances, this congregation is doing everything it can to remain viable. We all know that. It's common knowledge. And if you're implying it's Pastor Teschendorf's fault that our attendance is down, shame on you. We have a fine pastor who feeds us regularly with Word and sacrament. He may not have a lot of gifts for doing evangelism, but we're not all gifted in the same way. We ought to be thankful to have a man of his caliber."

"I agree with Stan." It was a voice rarely heard. Burt spoke softly and without any hint of anger. "This conversation is getting ugly. I, for one, am very uncomfortable. It isn't right. The man's not even here to defend himself."

Mark was moved by Burt's loyalty. But he was far from being convinced that Pastor Teschendorf was not part of the problem. "We all know this conversation wouldn't even be happening if Pastor Teschendorf were here," argued Mark. "As uncomfortable as this makes us, it has to be discussed. There's just no vision for our congregation's programs, no road map, no plan, no training or equipping, no trust in our lay members to lead or confidence in them to let them do more of the work. We've collectively buried the *one talent* we've each been given instead of putting it to work. Somebody has to be held accountable. If anything, we should be talking with the congregation's voters about these issues. They have a right to know. Ned is only being honest when he says we're a dying church. You have no right to shame him for that, Stan. Who made you the judge?"

Stan knew better than to take his former business partner to task in front of the church council, but he was seething. This was not the first time he had heard Mark talk about Pastor Teschendorf in this way. But it was the first time that it had come up in a council meeting. "That's enough, Mark," roared Stan, hammering his fist on the conference table for emphasis. "This whole discussion is out-of-bounds. Our pastor is a hardworking servant. It's slanderous to suggest otherwise. This has got to stop right here and now. Someone has to stand up to those people who bad-mouth our pastor. I'm going to be recommending that the board of elders remove you from office, Mark."

The meeting ended in an unsettling silence. Each council member stepped out into the icy blast alone, emotionally battered and bruised.

Troops Amassed on the Border

In a stage of conflict that may be characterized as *the gathering storm,* more individuals are drawn into the discord. The conflict is now defined by a growing sense of *polarization.* James Q. Wilson defined this phenomenon as "an intense commitment to a candidate, a culture, or an idealology that sets people in one group definitively apart from people in another, rival group."[47] For many conflicted families, schools, businesses, and churches, the *elephant in the room* is disunity. Unity requires constant attention. People who have gathered in disparate camps regard those who support an opposing cause not only as wrongheaded but also corrupt and wicked. Then rhetoric intensifies and spills into the public forum.

Polarized by Adiaphora

The Bible acknowledges that opinions can sometimes differ widely and still be in line with God's will. Unless God has clearly commanded or forbidden a course of action, he permits us to formulate ideas, dream dreams, consider possibilities, and make some sanctified choices for ourselves. Actually, the list of decisions that fall into this category is quite formidable. God wants us to exercise our new-man discretion in many different ways. And each time we do so, it gives honor and glory to his name.

The theological teaching that addresses our Christian freedom is called the doctrine of *adiaphora*. It's a Greek word used by Christians to refer to things that are neither commanded nor forbidden by God. The group at Peace Lutheran Church that supports the concept of full-time Christian education (owning and operating a Christian school or a child care center) has made this Bible principle the cornerstone of its rationale. And they are right. God's Word does not give a precise description of how Christians are to instruct their children in God's Word. We are free to do so at home, through a Sunday school program, in a Christian school, even online. What the members of this group have forgotten is that the Bible teaching of adiaphora needs to be applied to real life with a great deal of charity. If love is not part of the equation, their hearts are in the wrong place and they are not honoring God's name.[48] Instead, they have demanded the right to exercise their freedom. And they have taken advantage of those individuals who were confused about the distinction that must be made between the commands of God and the influences of culture and tradition.

The *Don't-Judge Principle*

The members who oppose the school do not seem to be willing to find better program alternatives, but they have become obstinate and stubborn and have decided that if they cannot get their own way, they will make it very difficult for the rest of the congregation to move forward. Some have even decided to withhold their offerings—a decision that will be construed as unloving and willful, neither of which are God-pleasing attitudes. Their attitudes will correctly be interpreted as judgmental and lacking patience. That is precisely the message they are hoping to send.

God does not want us to be the judges of the sincerity or motives of others. Jesus said, "Do not judge, or you too will be judged" (Matthew 7:1). And the apostle Paul told the Christians in Rome to "accept [those] whose faith is weak, without passing judgment on disputable matters" (Romans 14:1).[49]

A few individual members of Peace Lutheran Church are still hoping peace can prevail. Some will argue that the issues are too complex to be effectively handled internally. Most of the leadership team has already been compromised by entrenched positions. Others will contend that it is unwise to hang dirty laundry where everyone can see it. In any case, the body's future survival is clearly the main focus. In terms of individual souls, losses are incalculable and generally ignored.

A Numbers Game

As alliances coalesce around either pole, individuals are emboldened to articulate personal grievances. Old offenses resurface like zombies resurrected from an ancient graveyard. The most cogent can be used to generate the traction necessary for sustaining either side's sense of momentum. This battle-ready strategy is designed to attract the support of any remaining neutrals. Numbers have more significance now.

This is also the time for steeling the resolve of those warriors who will soon be ready to risk everything for their cause. The proverbial line in the sand has already been established. Its only purpose is symbolic—a justification for going to war. Meaningful dialog is shutting down. Conversations are being held in secret now or in hushed tones. They are more restricted. The only meaningful dialog occurs within the privacy of the two respective alliances. In the church setting, there may also be a good deal of pious talk aimed at securing the high moral ground—another effort to recruit uncommitted members.

Meaningful dialog is shutting down. Conversations are held in secret now, within the privacy of the two respective alliances.

One by one, individuals on both sides are undergoing a radical transformation—one that changes hearts at peace into hearts at war.

Early engagements strategically test the other side's resolve. A heightened aura of importance is placed on these early skirmishes in order to create a sense of urgency. Stan's declaration to seek Mark's removal from office may be such a test. It's a signal that the time has come to translate angry words into tangible actions.

We may have a hard time believing that any of this can be true of a Christian community. Yet for those who have actually experienced it in their own lives, sad memories of situations like the one just described may remain painfully real.

At this very moment, Satan is targeting some of our churches, schools, paraministry organizations, and Christian households for conflict. He has calculated the damage to faith life and ministry. He knows that fragile souls can be claimed for hell before the smoke clears from the battlefield.

Victors, Not Victims

Ask some of the more aware members of Peace Lutheran *what* is happening to their church and *why*. The range of opinions you are likely to get will vary widely. One person may point to the fact that the church is located in a changing neighborhood and it's getting harder to find parking nearby. Another argues that the congregation's financial woes won't get better until the economy improves or people learn to give more. A third observes that two strong-willed factions in the congregation are vying for control. Someone may politely whisper that the pastor's style doesn't seem to attract young families. Other members hint that the congregation's worship format is a little out of sync with the times or that the church's people need to be more involved in community service projects so that the church can develop a reputation for having members who are caring and compassionate. A knowing teenager may just shrug his shoulders, roll his eyes, and mumble, "Stuff happens!" Each unique view is probably rooted in some version of reality. But in spite of this conspicuous diversity, there is a common thread that runs through all of their perspectives. And it doesn't matter which side of the division they support or even if they are aware that a division exists. All of these people see themselves as *victims*.

Victim mentality and conflict often go hand in glove. In the fog of war, we can't see things clearly. It is especially easy to focus on the injustice that has been done to us. The knee-jerk reaction to injustice is to assume the role of the victim. The Arbinger Institute's insightful bestseller *The Anatomy of Peace* describes the phenomenon this way:

> Most who are trying to put an end to injustice only think of the injustices they believe they themselves have suffered. Which means that they are concerned not really with injustice but with themselves. They hide their focus on themselves behind the righteousness of their outward cause.[50]

A few individuals caught in the crosshairs of the conflict at Peace Lutheran Church may have ideas about how to help the congregation emerge from the shadows. But in the stifling environment of a war zone, storm clouds remain fixed in the background, threatening to disrupt any attempts at progress. In a dynamic that is locked and loaded with victim mentality, a peaceful resolution will be even more elusive.

Jesus does not want us to see ourselves as victims. None of his teachings suggests that we should view the world in which we live through the eyes of someone who is powerless. The concept itself is completely foreign to the mission he came to accomplish. It is inconceivable that the One who willingly carried our cross to his death ever played the victim's role. Victims have no say. They are unable to stop the aggression perpetrated against them. Jesus was fully in charge and in control, even when it didn't look that way.[51] Though he submitted to

Pontius Pilate's crushing judgment, Jesus was clearly not Pilate's victim.[52] Though he was placed on trial and convicted by an arrogant Sanhedrin, it would be wrong to cast him as their victim. Nor was he the victim of poverty, lies, or hatred, though he suffered all three. It's a simple truth, but so important: Christ Jesus was never the victim of human will.[53] His life on earth was his choice.[54] His suffering was his choice.[55] His death was his choice.[56]

Need proof? Look to the victory celebration of the resurrection. He defeated sin and crushed the evil one. He overcame death. He conquered hell. With the power of his forgiveness and love, Jesus triumphed over our cruel and wicked world, where people victimize one another as a common everyday occurrence.[57] And that is how he wants us to see ourselves: as *victors,* not victims.

For Thought and Discussion

- Explain why the kind of conflict that Peace Lutheran Church is experiencing cannot be dismissed as normal or acceptable behavior in a Christian congregation.

- Read the following statement. Then answer the question.

  The Lutheran church's teaching known as *adiaphora* rests in the biblical truth that God blesses his people with a free will to make choices about things that he has neither commanded nor forbidden in his Word. When we exercise our will in a God-pleasing (sanctified) way, we bring glory and honor to his name. The choice to own and operate a school falls under this definition of adiaphora, as do many other decisions, such as worship styles, the choice of individual cup in Communion, immersion or sprinkling in Baptism, and a host of other choices that congregations must make in their day-to-day exercise of ministry. This does not mean that such decisions are not important. Nor does it mean that people should not express their passionate views about whether it is wise to support one position or the other. It does, however, mean that, in love, we do not engage in bringing a moral judgment on anyone who holds an opinion that differs with our own.

In *The Shepherd Under Christ,* by Armin W. Schuetze and Irwin J. Habeck, we read, "A congregation may proceed to excommunication only when a sin is involved, never in the case of adiaphora (e.g., refusal to participate in a fundraising drive, refusal to send children to a Christian school, refusal to accept election or appointment to a congregational office or committee). Where admonition has taken place because of doctrinal deviation, only those are to be excommunicated who persistently adhere to an error which subverts the foundation of faith. . . . In other cases, separation is called for (Titus 3:10), i.e., the declaration that the persistent errorist is no longer a confessional brother, but not that he is to be regarded as a heathen man and a publican" (NPH, 1974, page 179).

Would the dynamics of this conflict be different if the cause for the division were a doctrinal matter instead of tension over an *adiaphoron?*

- In what ways can a pervasive *victim mentality* shape the direction of a Christian congregation?

PART TWO

Blessed Are the Peacemakers

Blessed are the peacemakers, for they will be called sons of God.

MATTHEW 5:9

A Parable[*]

By proclamation, the day of the royal wedding had been declared a *Day of All Days*.

The cathedral was filled to overflowing. Candlelight bathed its cavernous interior. Polished and festooned in a crimson military waistcoat, the groom stood proudly at the center of a massive chancel, his eyes riveted on the long aisle that divided the nave. A brace of handsomely outfitted escorts attended him. Banners bearing his crest fluttered from stonework arches that spanned the length of two parallel colonnades.

A magnificent pipe organ brought guests to their feet.

Each strained to catch a glimpse of the beauty for whose hand the brave champion had soldiered so valiantly.

At the distant opposite end of the aisle, a haggard female figure emerged from the shadows, her gown tattered and mud stained. She lurched, dazed and unstable. Welts marred her swollen face. Blood trickled from one nostril. Nearly closed, her left eye was encircled in luminous purple. A laceration oozed dark red from a matted patch of scalp.

The specter limped forward, supporting herself against a pew butt, then lunged forward to the next, gathering strength at each oasis for another desperate foray in the direction of her gentle monarch.

The guests were mortified. Groomsmen studied the floor. The organist stopped playing. All mourned silently for the faithful and heroic prince who deserved better. His bride had been fighting again. Yet, in a gesture of compassion, he strode the full length of the aisle to greet her. When he arrived at her side, he offered her his arm for support and smiled to reassure her of his enduring commitment.

*Based on the biblical picture of the church as the bride of Christ that the apostle Paul described in Ephesians 5:22-33.

The Peacemaker's Calling

There is a section of verses that appears early in Matthew's gospel known as the *Beatitudes* or the *Blessed Ares*.[58] They are part of Jesus' *Sermon on the Mount*. These poetic thoughts are unmatched for their comfort and encouragement. Jesus addresses them to believers like you and me.[59] His message is profoundly intimate and personal. To this day Christians the world over return to these precious sayings to rediscover their capacity to provide refreshment and renewal.

> *Blessed are* the poor in spirit, for theirs is the kingdom of heaven.
>
> *Blessed are* those who mourn, for they will be comforted.
>
> *Blessed are* the meek, for they will inherit the earth.
>
> *Blessed are* those who hunger and thirst for righteousness, for they will be filled.
>
> *Blessed are* the merciful, for they will be shown mercy.
>
> *Blessed are* the pure in heart, for they will see God.
>
> ***Blessed are* the peacemakers, for they will be called sons of God.**

> *Blessed are* those who are persecuted because of righteousness, for theirs is the kingdom of heaven.
>
> *Blessed are* you when people insult you, persecute you and falsely say all kinds of evil against you because of me. Rejoice and be glad, because great is your reward in heaven, for in the same way they persecuted the prophets who were before you.

As you just read Jesus' *Blessed Ares,* did you notice how powerfully they counter the temptation to play the role of the victim? How blessed we are in the endless flow of gifts that pour forth daily from a God who loves us and would do anything for us! To be so incredibly blessed, one can only come to the conclusion that he or she has triumphed over every adversary and overcome every obstacle to secure the ultimate victory. One can hardly be blessed in such abundance and still play the victim's role. As members of God's army of believers, we are winners. The apostle Paul wrote about the *victor-not-victim mentality* in similarly positive language to the congregation in Rome, where people were being martyred for their faith in Christ.

> We know that in all things God works for the good of those who love him, who have been called according to his purpose. . . . What, then, shall we say in response to this? If God is for us, who can be against us? He who did not spare his own Son, but gave him up for us all—how will he not also, along with him, graciously give us all things? Who will bring any charge against those whom God has chosen? It is God who justifies. Who is he that condemns? Christ Jesus, who died—more than that, who was raised to life—is at the

> right hand of God and is also interceding for us. Who shall separate us from the love of Christ? Shall trouble or hardship or persecution or famine or nakedness or danger or sword? As it is written: "For your sake we face death all day long; we are considered as sheep to be slaughtered." No, in all these things we are more than conquerors through him who loved us.[60]

The message of Jesus' *Blessed Ares* penetrates deep into the conflicted hearts of sinner-saints like us. Over and over, we are blessed. We have it all![61] Eternal life. Sure hope. Complete forgiveness. Heaven's glory. Lives with meaning and purpose. God's friendship and love. Transcendent peace. But why?

Well, we certainly do not deserve it. In a fair and objective court of law, you and I would deserve just the opposite. We fight. We argue. We murder, slander, abuse, and curse anyone who dares to cross us. We are sinners—failures when it comes to meeting God's expectations for perfection from the creatures who bear his image.[62] We ought to be cast into the fury of everlasting hatred. Yet in his grace, God has refused to let us become the victims of our own sinful hearts. We are his people, and he fought for us to the death, substituting his Son's flawless life for ours.

Did you also notice that at least one of these extraordinary *Blessed Ares* is of special interest for battle-wearied, walking wounded like us? *"Blessed are the peacemakers, for they will be called sons of God."* That thought ought to resonate, or at least raise a serious question or two. For starters, who are these people—these so-called peacemakers? And why are they being singled out for such high commendation? Membership in God's royal family is no small matter. His offspring will get special treatment. Their Father's servants are at their beck and call. Wouldn't you like to meet one of these *peacemakers,* so blessed to be counted among his heirs—inheritors of the royal heavenly realm?

You won't have to go too far to find one. Jesus was talking about you. Are you a little surprised? Not many of us readily recognize ourselves in Jesus' words. We know too much about the warlike thoughts that occupy our minds and the hatred that can take control of our hearts. Peacemaking is a little out of our league. Yet, Jesus here gives us a unique snapshot of our new-man selves as we are now, even in this earthly realm.

Peacemaking is a little out of our league. We know too much about the hatred that can take control of our hearts.

Peacemaker is yet another facet of our new identity in Christ Jesus. It is actually the title Jesus wants us to proudly carry with us everywhere we go. We are his peacemakers—people who are committed to carrying out the "ministry of reconciliation" that Paul wrote about. David Valleskey writes, "*'The ministry of reconciliation'* is the way by which God gets the message of reconciliation out into the world. God has made us missionaries."[63]

At the moments of our conversions, God transformed us into his imperial *peacemakers.* A major change—*for the good*—has occurred within our hearts. We are Spirit driven. And we continue to grow and become more like our Savior. We know the mission: Preach the peace of God's love to a dying world. Others are going to be blessed because we've been blessed as God's emissaries of peace. The apostle Paul laid out the whole plan in detail in 2 Corinthians, chapter 5:

> If anyone is in Christ, he is a new creation; the old has gone, the new has come! All this is from God,

> who reconciled us to himself through Christ and gave us the ministry of reconciliation: that God was reconciling the world to himself in Christ, not counting men's sins against them. And he has committed to us the message of reconciliation. We are therefore Christ's ambassadors, as though God were making his appeal through us. We implore you on Christ's behalf: Be reconciled to God. (verses 17-20)

Reconciliation comes from the Greek root word *katallasso*. In earlier Greek literature, this word was usually used in reference to a merchant *exchanging for equivalent values*. By the time Paul was using this word in his letters to New Testament congregations, its meaning had morphed into an expression that indicated a change in relationship. The change being expressed in 2 Corinthians 5:17ff. occurs in the dramatic shift from a relationship between us and God that was inherently hostile to one of peace and friendship. Jesus' work triggered this change. For sinners, his cross changes our guilty plea to NOT GUILTY. For unbelievers (as we also once were), the hope that comes from hearing God's promises changes dead hearts of stone to hearts alive with faith and eager to do God's will.

This change from the old Adam to the new man in Christ gives us a whole new outlook on many things. And it is responsible for the new views we have toward conflict and peacemaking.

We came into this world with a heart at war with God himself.[64] In Christ that has changed, so even as we are at peace with God because we are covered with Jesus' blood, we are also now Jesus' *peacemakers*—his movers and shakers. People of influence. Agents of change. Salt.[65] Light.[66] Yeast to change the bloodlust dynamic of a violent world with God's gospel of peace.[67] God works through us to make a difference, to make things happen in people's lives. Good things! Peaceful things!

In preparation for our peacemaking service, we've been washed and purified in the Lamb's innocent blood. The good news of our forgiveness (washing) in Christ is our hope—the very air that we breathe.

But that same gospel is also our purpose for having an ongoing conversation with the world in which we live. We are here to proclaim the life-transforming good news of God's promise for eternal peace to anyone within earshot. We've been authorized and certified to carry this divine policy of hope to the world. We carry the King's seal and his letter of protection. The tasks he has assigned to us were prepared before time began.[68] And the greatest joy of it all is that Jesus himself is right there at the center. All that has happened, is happening, or will happen is in Christ, through Christ, and in response to Christ's work for us. David P. Scaer explained it this way:

> Especially in his suffering and death, Jesus fits the description of the poor in spirit, those who mourn, the meek, those who hunger and thirst for righteousness, the merciful, the pure in heart, the peacemakers, and those who are persecuted for the sake of righteousness. . . . [These] Beatitudes are first Christological descriptions of Jesus, then descriptions of his followers. . . . Jesus' suffering will effect God's righteousness for [his followers], and they in turn will suffer for him and be rewarded by God in heaven.[69]

For my new man, fashioned in the likeness of Christ himself, there is nothing left to want. What more could I possibly still desire?[70] I am in the King's favor. And as I become more like my Savior, I discover that I have new wants that are no longer captive to my old sinful desires that have caused so much conflict and heartache.[71] I have the power to change my own attitudes and think about life's purpose in a way that is very different from the way my old Adam approached life. In my new-man life, I am filled with a new zeal for serving my Savior-God in the same selfless way that Jesus gave himself to the world of sinners. "God is already at peace with the world, and those who hear his Gospel must, like God, be at peace with one another and even with the community's avowed enemies."[72] We are now willing to share the burdens and trials that others face. It's a whole new lifestyle that engages us in a new kind of battle in which, like Christ himself, we will appear as victims but triumph in the end.[73]

This unexpected honor is ours the moment water and Word come together in Holy Baptism. In Baptism God calls us into his family of believers. From that moment on, his Spirit is constantly working with us to help us better understand the peacemaker's role that we've been given. We are never to see our new peacemaker's role as a part-time endeavor in which one can be on duty some of the time and off duty when it is more convenient to let an at-war heart operate with impunity. Nor is it one of those public ministry positions given to some of God's people and not to others. We are all God-certified peacemakers, whether we choose to carry out the mission we've been given or not.

Seeing ourselves as victors instead of victims radically changes our attitudes about conflict and the peacemaking role to which God has called us. It inspires us to gratefully accept this role and live lives of self-sacrifice and service. In doing so, we begin to imitate God and his great love for us[74] and carry the cross that Jesus has given us with joy and thanksgiving.[75]

Does this mean that we are all equally gifted for the work of peacemaking? No, just as we are not equally gifted for teaching or doing evangelism.[76] But it does mean that everyone carrying the imprint of the Savior on his or her heart will work at becoming a peacemaker. It further means we can expect to be called upon to exercise our peacemaking skills whenever opportunities arise. God wants us at the ready.[77]

For the members of Peace Lutheran Church, it means each member has a personal stake in moving the congregation forward toward a peaceful resolution. As one by one they begin to realize that God has called each of them to participate in the peacemaking endeavor, they will also begin to realize the resolution they are seeking is more about their faith life than their church's fiscal shortfall or their differences regarding the school's declining enrollment.

Being chosen to serve as one of God's peacemakers is an honor—a blessing among so many others. The leaders at Peace Lutheran Church may still decide to hire a professional interventionist—someone with tons of skills and plenty of training and experience. They may need the help of such an individual to navigate the troubled waters of their conflicted relationships. But the most skilled interventionist in the world will be doomed to failure if the members are unable to recognize how critical they are to creating a new culture in which peace and unity have a chance to prevail. Over the weeks and months ahead, each member will need to learn to see himself or herself as one honored with God's call to serve as a peacemaker in his kingdom.

The shift takes place when members no longer see themselves as victims and begin to see themselves as conquerors. It suggests a strategy that aims at moving members from their victim-orientation to an orientation that is rooted in their call to serve as God's peacemakers. When Christians are able to envision themselves in their new-man roles, good things will begin to happen. In his popular book *The Theology of the Cross,* Daniel Deutschlander writes:

> Instead of arrogance or self-righteousness, instead of depression or despair, the Christian has reason to rejoice beyond all measure because of the reality of his status. The Christian is a saint and child of God, a brother or sister of Christ and an heir of everlasting life. . . . That status is the reality. It is not a status yet to be earned or achieved. It is not a status that is merely potential, a possibility only gained by the best of us and not real until we get to heaven. . . . It is ours right now! . . . If I can just keep that reality in mind, what respect, what dignity, what honor you have in my eyes! To use you or take advantage of you for my own ends should never even occur to me. I wouldn't dream of hurting you or harming you. I cannot imagine speaking ill of you or insulting you. My fondest ambition is only this: to love and serve you.[78]

For Thought and Discussion

- What are the key steps that the apostle Paul describes for us in 2 Corinthians 5:17-20, explaining *how* and *why* God has called us to be his ambassadors of peace?

- How do Jesus' words recorded in Matthew 16:24 shape your thinking about being a called peacemaker in God's kingdom?

- What are the pros and cons of seeking outside intervention for a family or an organization embroiled in conflict?

CHAPTER 9

Conflict and Faith

The topic was *faith.* It had punctuated the disciples' conversations for months. And their discussions had been augmented by a handful of disturbing field experiences that exposed them as lightweights on the subject.

Understanding faith was quintessential to grasping the rest of Jesus' teachings. He talked about it all the time. But that is also what made the concept so troublesome. The harder these men tried to live the life of faith, the more miserably they failed. And the more they failed, the more elusive (and contentious) the topic became, until their debate had become quite personal. That was a good thing.

But their dialog was further complicated by the fact that it was framed in language that welcomed a comparison between mediocre faith and faith that deserved to be labeled *great.* These men were not spiritually mature enough to rise above playing the kinds of games *(Who's on Top?)* that compared their status with the status of others. But Jesus did not seem to mind the comparisons. In fact, he actually fostered the idea, pointing to exceptional models of faith among the people they encountered in their day-to-day travels. This made their comparisons all but inevitable.

Models of *Great* Faith

A woman who had been suffering from constant bleeding for more than a decade approached Jesus in a crowd and touched the hem of his cloak. She believed he had the power to cure her illness. Jesus acknowledged the woman's great faith, and she went away healed.[79]

Another woman—not a Jew but a Canaanite—came to Jesus to get help for her daughter. The girl was hopelessly controlled by a demon. The rigor with which Jesus tested the woman's conviction seemed almost harsh. But she passed with flying colors. In the end, the Lord held up her faith as a great example for others to emulate.[80]

A Roman centurion—a convert to Judaism—had come to Jesus, asking him to heal his dying servant. When Jesus offered to come to the centurion's house, the man replied, "Just say the word, and my servant will be healed." Jesus declared he had not witnessed a greater faith in all of Israel.[81]

The disciples wondered why the faith of these strangers was so much greater than theirs.

A few embarrassing experiences added to their sensitivities. None, for example, would ever forget the night they were crossing the Sea of Galilee in a tiny fishing boat when a deadly squall swept in from the West. Fierce winds and the tempestuous surf threatened to wash them overboard. There was every reason to panic. All the while Jesus lay curled up in the prow of the boat, sleeping. Beside themselves with anxiety, the disciples awakened him, pleading for his help. Before calming the wind and quieting the waves, Jesus chided them for having such weak faith.[82]

Another stormy night, Peter found an opportunity to demonstrate how strong his own faith had grown. Again while crossing the Sea of Galilee, the disciples saw an apparition walking on top of the water. They could tell that the figure was moving toward them. Occurrences of this kind were especially unnerving in their superstitious culture. Once again the men trembled in sheer terror. It turned out that what they saw was not a spirit-ghost at all; it was the master. He calmed their faint hearts by speaking to them across the water. They quickly recognized his voice and were encouraged.

Whether driven by his characteristic bravado or an abiding faith in God's loving power to watch over him, Peter climbed out of the boat and began walking toward Jesus with nothing but water beneath his feet. Then he lost his confidence and started to sink. When he cried out for help, Jesus held out his hand and lifted Peter up, saving him from certain drowning. When Peter caught his breath, Jesus asked him why he had let doubt shake his faith.[83] It was a sobering question, acutely personal for Peter.

Then a man brought his demon-possessed son to the disciples. We aren't told why the father did not go directly to Jesus. Perhaps the crowds were so large that the desperate man feared he might never get close enough to Jesus to get the help he needed. Whatever the reason, some of the disciples thought they might be up to the task of taking on a demon. They were wrong. When they later asked Jesus why they were unable to cast the demon out of the boy, he told them the truth: their faith was *too small*.[84] In the wake of such disappointments, some of them finally found the nerve to come right out and ask, "Who is the greatest in the kingdom of heaven?" (Matthew 18:1).

The question itself is worth some reflection. For starters, the word *faith* does not appear in the question. Though faith was clearly at the heart of the matter, the disciples' were still having difficulty understanding how to measure *greatness* from God's perspective. In every kingdom they could imagine, greatness was always and inevitably self-directed and self-glorifying; it had nothing to do with humility.

We are also left with the impression that their question had been edited to avoid any of the prickly tensions smoldering just beneath the surface.[85]

Jesus knew about the tension, and he was prepared to deal with it. He had been waiting for the right moment to teach them a foundational lesson about the nature of faith. That moment had finally arrived.

The Lesson

Jesus asked the master of the house to send his youngest child into the room. He wanted his followers to think about the unique qualities of *childhood*. It was a good way to focus their attention. Childhood is a universal human experience. But Jesus also understood that adults quickly forget what childhood is like. His disciples were grown men. They needed a visual aid to help them remember.

Soon a toddler stood before them. It was obvious he had no claim to greatness. No money. No job. No education. No experience. No authority. No priceless information. No pedigree. No physical strength to speak of. No royal title. No valuable possessions. No impressive body of knowledge. No plan. No academic degree. No skills. No special connections. No unique powers. No notoriety or fame. No resources of any kind. Matthew does not even bother to tell us the child's name. In the *who's who* of their day, the youngster mattered so little that he didn't even have an identity of his own. In plain English, the lad was a *nothing, a nobody*—completely reliant on others to sustain, support, and nurture him.

The lecture began. "I tell you the truth," said Jesus, "unless you change and become like little children, you will never enter the kingdom of heaven. Therefore, whoever humbles himself like this child is the greatest in the kingdom of heaven" (Matthew 18:3,4).

It took a moment for the gravity of Jesus' words to sink in. Suddenly there was a lot more at stake here than personal pride. It is impossible to trump words like *unless* or *never*. He had their attention. Eternity hung in the balance; this lesson was about their eternal future.

But it was the twice-referenced *kingdom of heaven* that gave them a real cause to pause. It was one of those major themes woven into so many of Jesus' monographs. He was challenging them. They needed to see the radical contrast between the kingdoms of this world and the spiritual realm in which he was operating.

History tells us that some of the kingdoms of the past were truly remarkable. The Medes and Persians. The Assyrian Empire. Ancient Babylon. The Egyptian dynasties. Alexander the Great. The Roman Empire. The British Empire. The Mongolian Empire. The Holy Roman Empire. The Ming Dynasty. Each had its day in the sun. We still admire them. One excelled in law, another in military might. Some were political juggernauts; some, cultural giants. Others were known for technological innovation, trade, or organized government. Each left a footprint. And each footprint was eventually washed into oblivion by the tides of time.

We carve niches, climb corporate ladders, set goals, develop skills, work the system, and make the effort to build our own personal Babels. Our kingdoms matter.

We pursue another kind of kingdom in our day-to-day lives. Some of us invest our time and energy in the kingdoms of medicine or law. Or we make our marks in mass media, agriculture, the arts, commerce, technology, education, government, or the church. We carve niches, climb ladders, and set goals to build our own personal Babels.[86] Our kingdoms matter. Each of us would like to have our day of greatness in whatever kingdom we've had a hand in building.

At a deeply personal level, many of us engage in the establishment of yet another very private kingdom. This kingdom is all about *my* talent, *my* career, *my* honor, *my* beliefs, *my* status, *my* image, *my* legacy, *my* influence, *my* ideas, *my* successes, *my* intellect, *my* perspective. It can also include *my* family, *my* church, *my* school, *my* job, *my* country, etc. We've been working at perfecting this kingdom most of our adult lives, convinced it will brand us with a public identity that is at once noteworthy and favorable. We protect this kingdom and flaunt it, enlarge it and control it, refine it and utilize it to bring glory and honor to ourselves. We will die for it if necessary. It is a fragile kind of kingdom that depends entirely on us. Without our constant attention it will quickly disintegrate.

The child standing there before Jesus and his disciples had no kingdoms to build, nor did he give even the most casual thought to such a lifelong endeavor. He was happy just *to be,* satisfied with the nurture, support, and love that his parents gave him. In this way he was genuinely humbled by his status as a child. He lived with assumptions: someone will help me; someone will protect me; someone will care for my needs; someone will do for me what I am unable to do for myself. These unspoken convictions shaped his entire worldview, including that part of his worldview reserved for dealing with conflict.

For a Christian, the power for dealing with conflict is faith. You and I need the humility of that child, trusting

God to provide whatever resources we will need to replace hearts hell-bent on making war with hearts eager to live in peace. We need the example of God's love for us (remember that we were born enemies of God[87]) to move us to forgive people who have brought untold misery, heartache, and pain into our lives. We need that child's confidence to rely on our heavenly Father to provide all that we need to sustain our lives so that we do not obsess over wanting. We need his humble integrity so that simple truth does not become distorted by our own self-serving point of view. We need his humility, which leaves the judging of the behaviors of others to the eternal Judge who has the authority to condemn wrongful thoughts, words, and deeds. We need to become like that little boy, completely satisfied with being a child of God and not the least bit concerned with lording over his adversaries. The age-old pattern that leads Christians into wrongheaded conflict can be overcome. But it will require the simple and humble faith of a child.

Faith trusts in Jesus to justify us before the eternal Judge. Faith clings to the Father's promise to forgive when we have cursed a family member, destroyed a coworker's reputation, slandered a neighbor, or harbored murderous thoughts toward someone who has hurt us. Faith pleads for God's help and strength when temptation is stalking us. Faith gives us a reason to hope for a miracle to end our conflicts and restore the peace. Why? Because faith itself is nothing short of a miracle.

The apostle Paul knew about childlike faith. He once referred to himself as the greatest of sinners.[88] That's a humble perspective. But he also recognized that his strength to rise up and conquer the real enemy came from God. "I will boast all the more gladly about my weaknesses," he wrote, "so that Christ's power may rest on me.

That is why, for Christ's sake, I delight in weaknesses, in insults, in hardships, in persecutions, in difficulties. For when I am weak, then I am strong" (2 Corinthians 12:9,10). When peace seems like a pipe dream, we not only need to recognize our weaknesses, we need to glory in them. Only then can we turn to God for the strength we lack.

An Outrageous Illustration

Before we leave this powerful image of that child shyly standing before Jesus' followers, we must wrestle with one final aspect of Jesus' lesson. Consider once again what he said: *"Unless you change and become like little children . . ."* Does this strike you as a cockeyed notion? For practical people, such a thing is clearly outside the box of human experience. If Jesus Christ had not said it, these words would have been dismissed long ago as the words of a fool or a madman. Not in the entire history of our planet has a single case ever been reported in which an adult has miraculously returned to his or her childhood. It's like the virgin birth or being born again. Hollywood loves such crazy notions just because they are so impossible. Anyone with an ounce of common sense knows this kind of thing isn't going to happen, not in our lifetimes or anyone else's. Worse, because such a thing is humanly impossible, Jesus' message, if misunderstood, could lead us to despair. Given the scientific facts, we must conclude that for those of us who have already reached our adult years, heaven is out of reach. Who among us has the power to return to that time of our lives when we were children? We adults have all tasted the kingdom-building poison. We're in the process right now of building our towers in Babel to make a name for no one other than *moi*. We've been conditioned to be independent and self-reliant. There is no turning back.

And that's the whole point! Only God can make such impossible things happen. What we cannot do, God does. Through the miracle of his Holy Spirit, we can—and we do—become childlike, completely reliant on God's charity and goodwill for everything we need. In God's kingdom, the greater one's faith, the more that person depends on God's grace and the less that person relies on his or her own resources. And, yes, Jesus wants each of us to grow in our faith until that day when we can move mountains . . . or do the hard things that resolving conflict requires.[89] Faith sets a Christian's approach to conflict resolution apart from the conflict-resolution approaches of secular strategies. With faith one can accomplish the impossible.

For Thought and Discussion

- Read Mark 9:14-29. Focus on the words spoken by the boy's father in verse 24: "I do believe; help me overcome my unbelief!" In the light of that father's confession, how do you measure up with regard to your faith in God's promises?

- Secular resources do not speak about faith as an important ingredient in resolving conflict (except, perhaps, in terms of putting one's confidence in a strategy or a process). Is our faith in Jesus really a difference maker? Explain.

CHAPTER 10

The Marks of a Peacemaker

Have you ever seen one of God's peacemakers in action? It's not hard to spot one in a crowded room. People, like us, who have been called into God's army of peacemakers are marked with characteristics that clearly identify us as his ambassadors of peace. Once again the apostle James makes an important contribution to our understanding of how we will want to see ourselves in the peacemaking role when the battle rages:

> He gives us more grace. That is why Scripture says: "God opposes the proud but gives grace to the humble." Submit yourselves, then, to God. Resist the devil, and he will flee from you. Come near to God and he will come near to you. Wash your hands, you sinners, and purify your hearts, you double-minded. Grieve, mourn and wail. Change your laughter to mourning and your joy to gloom. Humble yourselves before the Lord, and he will lift you up. (James 4:6-10)

Preparing our hearts and minds for engaging in the battles that God wants us to be waging is serious business. It is a humbling process that requires some personal soul-searching. But it is also the way that we grow into our God-given peacemaking role.

Jesus spoke of this process using a brilliant metaphor that anyone living in his day would have been able to understand. He explained that before we can be of any real help to others who are caught up in sin, we first have to recognize the flaws in our own lives and (in a spiritual sense) have these flaws (*sins*) surgically removed. He illustrated the point with a picture of two people who had both managed to get something caught in their eyes. Perhaps Jesus was reflecting on his days as an apprentice growing up in Joseph's woodworking shop. To make his point, Jesus stretched the metaphor to the point of being unrealistic. One person had a speck in his eye. The other, who tried to help him, had a beam in his. The picture translates rather easily to the language of conflict resolution.

While it is a great honor to be called to serve as God's peacemaker, this role can be one of the most demanding and difficult tasks that God can call on us to do. Peacemaking is all about making the kinds of changes that can transform the dangerous dynamic of conflict into a dynamic that leads to peace and unity. But change at the high-stakes level of conflict resolution is never an easy thing to accomplish. Locked in combat, people's hearts are generally only interested in bringing about a major change in their enemy's status. But sin is involved in conflict. It is that sin we must address when we try to resolve conflict. Jesus' indignation flashes at the attitude that assumes the ability to remove the speck of sin from our brother's eyes without first dealing with the sin of two-by-four proportion in our own eyes.[90]

The first change that will need to be made will have to occur within. Would-be peacemakers need spiritual *I* surgery. *Before you do anything,* said Jesus, *you've got something there in your own eye—an obstruction, a hindrance, a block of some kind. You can see the hateful things that others do, but you are unable to see what you are capable of doing to others. It's hard enough to see things clearly when your sight is unobstructed. You can't be of much help to yourself or anyone else if you don't have that obstruction taken care of.* And since we can still sometimes revert to the promptings of our old Adam, the process is bound to be ongoing.

Peacemaking is about making the kind of changes that will transform hearts equipped for conflict into hearts that are committed to peace and unity.

Our Great Physician knows how to deal with the flaws and blockages in our lives. He's done plenty of similar surgeries. He sees our weaknesses clearly. He sees the godless things hidden in our hearts. If we are going to be of any use to Jesus, or anyone else, something will need to be done about that plank. Jesus is the right surgeon for the delicate job of removing the obstruction.

The bad news is that *I* surgery of this kind is painful and expensive. The hateful, noxious behaviors we've concealed over a lifetime will have to be removed. But here's the good news: Jesus has removed the offending blockage. The cost was priceless—his holy lifeblood. But the surgery was a complete success. We can now see ourselves in the mirror, warts and all. And we are humbled by what we see. In such humility, we can be of use to others without self-righteously judging them or speculating about their motives.

The secular world occasionally takes a page from Christianity and adapts a view that makes some sense, even if it isn't lined up with the cross. A quote from The Arbinger Institute's book on peacemaking gets this part right:

> A culture of peace can never be created by behavioral strategy alone. Peace—whether at home, work, or between peoples—is invited only when an intelligent outward strategy is married to a peaceful inward one. . . . If we don't get our hearts right, our strategies won't matter. . . . The essential foundation is change in ourselves.[91]

Unfortunately, the secular world has not yet discovered the surgeon's name who can do the surgical procedure that is needed for real healing to occur.

Two Conflict-Resolution Models

Every family—every congregation or parachurch organization—has its own way of dealing with tension and internal conflict. The adult thing to do is to get along with one another at some functional level. Most of us get that. Common disputes and disagreements need resolution. If they are not resolved, communication, coordination, and cohesion will begin to erode. The long-term effect can eventually become permanently debilitating.

Two models dominate the conflict-resolution landscape of our world. We'll call one model the *Therapy Model.* We will refer to the other as the *Forgiveness Model.*

Both models are attempts to restore broken relationships to a degree of peaceful coexistence. They both operate with the general principle that failure should never be considered as the first option. To paraphrase one conflict-resolution guru, *I can accept failure, but I cannot accept not trying.*[92] The ultimate goal of both models is to achieve a lasting resolution between disagreeing individuals. Both models can be, and are, used in environments that range far beyond the family, such as in the business world or in the school environment. Yet both are generally instilled in our worldviews at a fairly early age within the context of the family. One mom might intervene in a fight between her two children using a therapeutic approach while another mom intervenes using the forgiveness model.

The two models are not mutually exclusive. In some situations they can actually complement each other. But at a philosophical level, they are very different approaches to healing a relational breach. We might even say that in their purest forms, one conflict-resolution model is clearly God-pleasing and the other is not. And yet, it's not uncommon to find unbelievers using a version of the Forgiveness Model or Christians using some version of the Therapy Model. It would be wrong, for example, to suggest that no self-respecting secular psychologists would ever employ a secularized (Christ-less) version of the Forgiveness Model. In fact, many do.

And to be completely fair, there are some good things that can be said about the Therapy Model. For one thing, it works; or at least it works up to a point. People who are hurting and have struggled with the pain that comes with a broken relationship can find relief from their suffering through the therapeutic process. In many cases, personal therapy allows an individual to overcome issues that have damaged or destroyed trust in the party that has caused the damage. Furthermore, the Therapy Model does force people to consider the powerful impact past events can have on us. Therapy often forces conflicted individuals to come to grips with their personal history in ways that will help them better understand their pain. In fact, therapy can even help them find a way out of their pain.

At the heart of the Therapy Model is the assumption that a person can only take responsibility for his or her own actions. In other words, it assumes we have no control or influence over the thoughts or actions of another person. In a sense, the Therapy Model's strategy is to sidestep the rift in a relationship and unilaterally develop mechanisms that will make it possible to put the matter off to the side so that it cannot dominate or damage the person receiving the therapy. You've heard the expression "forgive and forget"; the Therapy Model is far more interested in teaching people how to forget. And the resources necessary for forgetting are generally seen as coming from within the individual.

The Therapy Model does not concern itself with actually wiping clean the slate of offenses perpetrated by either side. It does not really address the deeper need to somehow restore a broken relationship to its original, issue-free condition. It only changes the individual's frame of mind so that the issue itself has been unilaterally neutralized.

The Forgiveness Model is all about restoring relationships to their original, issue-free condition. The apostle Paul was speaking about the Forgiveness Model when he wrote to the Christians living in Corinth about the *message and ministry of reconciliation.* The Forgiveness Model's overriding aim is to heal the breach. It holds out the hope that each party might once again enjoy a healthy and thriving relationship that is based in trust and mutual love for each other. Its objective is to wipe both slates clean so that a fresh start can be made.

The Forgiveness Model is a reflection of the biblical model of reconciliation in which full and free forgiveness has been bought and paid for with Christ's own life. The power for wiping the slate of offenses clean does not come from within the individual. It comes from God himself. He has wiped our slates clean with the blood of his own dear Son.[93]

We forgive one another even as God, for Christ's sake, has forgiven us. We forgive without any strings attached. Forgiveness that is based on agape love is never a *quid pro quo* arrangement. Our forgiveness is not contingent on whether the other party decides to forgive us.

The biblical Forgiveness Model is the model that God has given to his people to restore unity and peace in broken relationships. It is the quintessential truth of the Christian faith. The real beauty of it is that it also has the capacity to heal broken hearts and once again give both parties a chance to minister to each other with gospel love.

Most families lean on the Therapy Model in one way or another, even if their members are all-confessing Christians. This model is manifested in the deal-with-it mentality so prevalent in today's society. The irony of the Forgiveness Model is that it transforms individuals who see themselves as victims into people who, in the act of forgiving an enemy, actually regain control of their own conflicted lives.

Marked by Courage

Let's not sugarcoat the *peacemaker* role you and I have acquired through our membership in God's family. From the world's way of looking at things, being an ambassador of peace in God's kingdom is filled with risk and fraught with danger. Jesus forewarned his disciples not to be surprised if their work would not always be appreciated. He used some strong language to prepare them for what they could expect: "All men will hate you because of me."[94] Those disciples, most of whom died a martyr's death, no doubt went to their graves with these words echoing in their ears.

At the height of Peace Lutheran Church's version of hell on earth, any member who would play the role of a peacemaker would surely be unpopular with some other members. Even when love is the motivation behind it, telling others the truth about their godless behaviors can quickly turn friends into enemies. When Paul felt compelled to admonish the Christians living in Galatia about the dangers of allowing themselves to once again be driven by the law, he recognized that his message might not be a welcomed one. You can sense the angst and heartache in his voice when he asked, "Have I now become your enemy by telling you the truth?" (Galatians 4:16).

It takes courage to stand in a place where anyone and everyone can get a clean shot at you. If humility is the first mark of a Christian peacemaker and the second mark is having the right model, then the third mark of God's peacemaker is courage. "Courage is not simply one of the virtues, but the form of every virtue at the testing point."[95] It is the kind of fearlessness that Jesus inspires in all of his followers with the reassuring words, *Don't be afraid. I am with you. You're not alone.*[96] "Jesus puts fear and faith at opposite ends of the spectrum: 'You of little faith, why are you so afraid?'"[97] He strengthens us for a noble battle in which souls are at stake and the prospect of victory is a sure thing. Isaiah, who lived in a combat zone most of his life, wrote,

> "Though the mountains be shaken and the hills be removed, yet my unfailing love for you will not be shaken nor my covenant of peace be removed," says the LORD, who has compassion on you.[98]

And the apostle Paul, who was once a murderer and a violent man,[99] wrote, "Be men [and women] of courage; be strong."[100]

For Thought and Discussion

- What is likely to happen if a person who is arrogant and self-righteous tries to correct someone who is caught in a cycle of sin?
- Why do you think the Therapy Model has so much appeal for people who are troubled by relational conflicts?
- Where do you go to find the encouragement and strength you need to do the truly difficult things in life?

CHAPTER 11

Power Tools for **Peacemakers**

Instinct tells us there are two ways to put a quick end to our conflict nightmares: *stand and fight* or *run the other way*. The truth is that when the fight-or-flight options are seen as one's only alternatives, you're dealing with an urban myth.

The fight response (which on Sande's illustration includes *murder, assault,* and *litigation*) generally increases hostility and exacerbates conflict.

The flight option (which on Sande's illustration includes *suicide, flight,* and *denial*), on the other hand, is self-directed. Running away from conflict or ignoring it can have the unhealthy effect of driving issues inward. When the causes for conflict remain unaddressed, raw emotions continue to fester within. Internalized conflict produces people who are living in despair over dead or imperiled relationships.

God has provided a range of powerful conflict-management tools and conflict-resolution strategies that are capable of producing results that are far more satisfying than fight-or-flight alternatives could ever hope to provide.

One option is simply to look the other way.

Don't dismiss this possibility too quickly or without some prayerful thought. Patience is a godly virtue. In a culture that is quick to take offense and often inclined toward a violent reaction, God's people can learn to overlook some of the incidental bad habits and obnoxious behaviors of others. Rudeness, for example, is never acceptable; but we can tolerate the insufferable behaviors of some, instruct others, and offer positive models to those who may not realize they are offending us.[101]

There are also those personalities that seem to thrive on making life miserable for others by remaining in a constant argumentative lather about something. They take special delight in sticking it to you at every opportunity. We all know the type, and many of us struggle with finding the patience to deal with such individuals in a loving way. It is almost as though God places such people into our lives for the express purpose of keeping us humble and teaching us temperance and forbearance. If you have such a person in your life, you may want to consider what lessons God is trying to teach you about yourself.

On the other hand, some of the causes for conflict cannot be overlooked. What then?

God has blessed the human race with several practical intervention strategies to effectively restore some level of peace to our conflict-ridden relationships. Three of these strategies are *mediation, negotiation,* and *arbitration.* Without these high-impact tools for managing crisis-level conflicts, society would soon slip into anarchy and chaos under the terrific weight of unresolved conflicts. So, we first need to recognize each as a valuable gift and a blessing in its own right.

Mediation

Mediation makes use of a neutral third party (a *mediator*) whose role is to clarify issues and keep the lines of communication open so that acceptable terms for making peace can eventually be achieved. Jesus Christ is our mediator with our divine Judge. He stands (like an Old Testament priest) as our go-between at the Father's throne of grace.[102] When we pray the words "in Jesus' name," we are remembering his role as our mediator with God.[103]

Negotiation

Negotiation involves trade-offs. Opposing parties agree to forfeit some claims in exchange for having other claims upheld. Divorce settlements often resort to a combination of mediation and negotiation as a way to bring some semblance of peace to an otherwise ugly situation. In this way, there can at least be some sense of closure.

Arbitration

In arbitration, the hostile parties actually agree to empower a neutral third party to settle a dispute for them. Honest civil courts and a fair system of jurisprudence can effectively intervene when disputes and disagreements threaten the peace.

But secular society has a bad habit of distorting public opinion regarding the Christian worldview. For that reason, biblical morality does not always play well in a secular court of law.

Litigation

In civil matters, Scripture urges us to seek resolution through the help of our fellow Christians in an effort to settle disputes out of court. The apostle Paul wrote:

> If any of you has a dispute with another, dare he take it before the ungodly for judgment instead of before the saints? Do you not know that the saints will judge the world? And if you are to

> judge the world, are you not competent to judge trivial cases? Do you not know that we will judge angels? How much more the things of this life! Therefore, if you have disputes about such matters, appoint as judges even men of little account in the church! I say this to shame you. Is it possible that there is nobody among you wise enough to judge a dispute between believers? But instead, one brother goes to law against another—and this in front of unbelievers!
>
> The very fact that you have lawsuits among you means you have been completely defeated already. Why not rather be wronged? Why not rather be cheated? Instead, you yourselves cheat and do wrong, and you do this to your brothers. (1 Corinthians 6:1-8)

Unimpeded by public opinion, armed with biblical principles, anchored in Christian love, and using the same gifts of negotiation, mediation, and arbitration, God's people are free to arrive at a fair-minded settlement out of the public's view.

There is another reason for Christians to settle their disagreements with one another out of court. People engaged in an intense conflict are tempted to use litigation to intimidate, punish, or gain leverage over an enemy. Conflicts come from a heart that is poisoned with *(1) wanting, (2) distorting the truth, (3) judging,* and *(4) punishing.* That is not the kind of heart we want driving our new-man-in-Christ decision about whether to take someone to court in a lawsuit. Western law makes a careful distinction between civil suits that are *compensatory* and those that are *punitive.* Old Testament civil law seems to support the concept of compensatory reimbursement.[104] Punitive suits, on the other hand, do not seem to have the same biblical support. Litigation can be used as a weapon. There is a danger that the motive to sue is driven by personal desire to punish an enemy. That's generally not a God-pleasing motive for taking someone to court. If you are contemplating a lawsuit, prayerfully examine your motives to learn more about *why* you are considering your legal option to sue. There is a huge difference between taking someone to court because it is your legal right to do so and taking someone to court because it is morally the right thing to do.

A Communication Model

The peacemaker's role requires several basic skills. Among the most important is the ability to communicate.

God takes a special interest in the way in which his people communicate. He understands communication. He created us to be social creatures. He gave us the gift of language. He reveals himself to us in his Word by speaking to us. He listens to us when we speak to him in prayer.

Effective communication, both in terms of speaking and listening—occurring within the four walls of a Christian home or among the members of a Christian congregation—should be a high priority. *What* we say and *how* we say it has the potential to encourage, support, comfort, and build up others. These outcomes are intrinsic to healthy Christian relationships. But the things we say to others also have the potential to discourage, frustrate, tear down, and destroy—any of which can either be the by-products or the causes of conflict.

Effective communication sets the stage for sharing the one thing that can bring joy, peace, and unity to anyone who hears us proclaiming the gospel. Failure to communicate effectively (at any level) will frustrate and impede the gospel's proclamation.

The principles of godly communication apply to every social setting and all human relationships. But they are especially applicable to life in the family setting. The home is where communication principles are first taught and practiced. Even if we don't always apply them, most of us understand the biblical imperatives for God-pleasing communication. They address the attitudes of the heart. And they are amazingly simple.

1. Be honest (Ephesians 4:25).
2. Encourage one another (1 Thessalonians 5:11).
3. Don't find fault with others or judge them (Matthew 7:1-5).
4. Keep your tongue under control (James 1:26).
5. Build others up instead of tearing them down (Romans 15:1,2).
6. Talk about things of lasting value—things worth treasuring (Philippians 4:8).

A Christian's whole life is governed by two additional principles—*love* and *forgiveness*. We are to "love one another deeply."[105] And we are to forgive one another.[106] In fact, every time we pray the Lord's Prayer, we are reminded to forgive others.[107] These are not platitudes to be hauled out and dusted off on special occasions. We express them in all of our actions and in the everyday things we say to one another.

A Reason to Listen

"Communication does not begin with being understood, but with first understanding others."[108] However, the principles for healthy listening are not always understood as well as the spoken component of our communication.

Healthy communication is a balance (though not necessarily a proportionate balance) of speaking and listening. Communication experts encourage us to listen in order to demonstrate respect for, and acceptance of, others. This is a fine principle. But a Christian's approach to listening represents more than a goodwill token. Respect for one another certainly is an attitude God wants us to cultivate.[109] But for peacemakers, the main point of listening is to learn what the speaker needs and how we can minister to those needs. Listening—active and engaged listening—gives us definitive clues to how we can do a better job of serving others.[110]

Our listening begins with a posture that invites "the other person into the conversation with us, to help us figure things out. If we are going to achieve our purposes, we have lots we need to learn from them and lots they need to learn from us. We need to have a *learning* conversation."[111]

It is virtually impossible to have meaningful dialog without an understanding of the facts. But fact-gathering requires basic skills and an inviting attitude. For example, it would be self-defeating for a listener to try to garner facts with a posture that projects "I already know all I need to know to understand what happened." Such a posture announces that you have already decided that you are right. Nor is it productive to assume a posture that projects "I know what you intended." That is an indication that you've already judged the person's motive as inappropriate or immoral.

It is likewise unproductive to leave the impression that the speaker's feelings are irrelevant and that it would not be helpful for the person to share how he or she feels. It sends a signal that this person's hurts don't really matter to you.[112] None of these postures are helpful for stimulating a conversation that reaches toward learning and growing in understanding. All of them send the message that you do not honor or respect the thoughts or feelings of the other person.[113] Such attitudes lack humility and project arrogance.

Listening is crucial to understanding. But the simple facts are not always *simple.* We all approach the events of our lives from a unique set of experiences and histories. We are uniquely gifted and hold divergent views of how the world should be. The facts as one person observes them are inexorably different from the way another observer will see the same facts. And we each interpret the same facts in a way that is unique.

What happened? is the right question to ask to begin probing for facts. Practiced listeners know how important it is to have the facts of a story communicated in the least emotional way. They understand that they may have to spend time and energy to calm an emotionally charged person so that facts can be conveyed accurately. That is why peacemakers will often frame their conversations with a reassuring prayer or Bible reading.

While fact-finding is generally interested in hearing a story unencumbered by expressions of human emotions, that is not to say our emotions have no place in productive dialog.

Once the story has been shared and the facts gathered, the emotional elements of the story also need to be expressed. While emotional output may range widely from one person to the next, the Creator constructed us in a way that actually demands emotional expression. Sorrow, fear, joy, shame, and anger need to be articulated. And it is not overstating the case to suggest that without opportunities to express feelings, it is unlikely that a learning conversation will be able to move to the next level. Good listeners patiently provide plenty of chances for venting. It is never wise to ignore this critical aspect of communication.

In the final phase, the listener begins to probe the fundamental question *why*. This part of active listening zeroes in on the heart of an issue because the question *why* examines personal beliefs. (Of a specific event, the question might be, *Why do you think this happened?*) The point is to gain a better understanding of how the speaker's grasp of the facts and emotional interpretation of the event are shaped by his or her experiences; his or her interpretations of the things seen, heard, smelled, tasted, or physically felt; and his or her understanding of relational tensions and strengths. Actually anything and everything that make up this person's being—including his or her religious beliefs and the personal trust he or she places in God, or gods, or himself or herself as the god being worshiped—contribute to this person's personal belief system. But don't be fooled; when we are hearing a person's beliefs, it will only be truth insofar as the person sees truth—it's *his or her* perception. The conclusions this person has drawn will inevitably reflect his or her self-interests. For sinners, that always presents a problem. Nevertheless, it is critical information that can lead a peacemaking ambassador to provide a tailor-made message of hope and comfort.

1. LISTEN: Focus on understanding.
   QUE: *Am I really listening?*
2. EXPERIENCE: Invite the person to tell a story.
   QUE: *What happened?*
3. FEELINGS: Provide opportunity to vent.
   QUE: *How do you feel about what happened?*
4. TRUTH: Invite the person to share convictions.
   QUE: *Why do you believe this happened?*

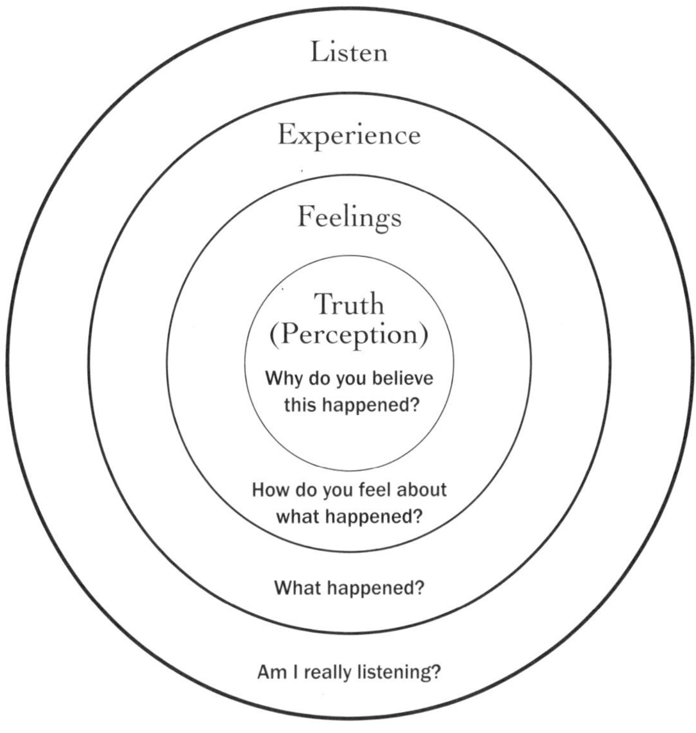

© Kenneth J. Kremer

The purpose of active listening ranges far beyond idle talk. We who know God's love in our own lives have something vital to offer others. And sometimes we just can't wait to share it. But conflict, you may recall, is a breeding ground for temptation and sin. A peacemaker needs to listen first to determine whether it is the right time to talk about God's expectations (law) and someone's failure to meet them or the right time to share the good news of God's love and forgiveness (gospel) with someone who is despairing over sin.[114] If our listening reveals an opportunity to share God's forgiveness, we may be able to help mend a broken heart with the gospel's reassuring and hopeful message.

Sometimes the conversation will also tell us if we are dealing with a sin of conscience or a sin of ignorance. If it is a sin of conscience, it will need to be addressed with careful rebuke. If it is a sin committed out of ignorance, it will rather be addressed with patient instruction. The objective always remains the same: spiritual growth.[115]

Careful listening can also uncover pain, fear, loneliness, confusion, or a host of other human emotions. It can help us understand how we can help carry someone else's burdens. It can lead us to a better understanding of the dangers and temptations people face as conflict intrudes in their lives.

Dostoevsky wrote, "One must have a heart to understand."[116] Peacemakers pray for discerning hearts that are filled with compassion for people who are hurting or for those who are about to hurt someone else. Active listening calls our attention to the unchecked emotions that often lead to conflict.

Combat With God

An event in the life of the Old Testament patriarch Jacob provides God's peacemakers with another important insight into how he wants us to approach personal conflict.

After Jacob had fled his childhood home to avoid the wrath of his brother, Esau, whom he had cheated out of the family birthright/blessing, he went to live at his uncle's place in Paddan Aram some 500 miles away. There Jacob's life seemed charmed. He worked hard. And God blessed him with a large family and great wealth.[117] But Jacob's estrangement from his brother, Esau, continued to haunt him. His plans always aimed for the day when he would return to his homeland. There he would have to face the sins of his past. And Jacob accepted that.

After 20 years in Laban's employ, Jacob packed up everything he owned and quietly slipped away, leading his entourage southwest, in the direction of his childhood home.

On the way, Jacob began to anticipate a worst-case scenario—a head-to-head battle for survival with his estranged brother. So he sent messengers ahead, seeking his brother's forgiveness and favor. But the messengers returned to report that Esau was bearing down on Jacob's camp with four hundred men.

Jacob's strategy was first to divide his camp into two parties, hoping that at least one group would escape Esau's army. Then he sent emissaries with wave after wave of gifts for his brother as peace offerings, hoping the relationship between the two of them could be reconciled.

On the eve of his anticipated clash with Esau, Jacob quietly moved his family and possessions across the Jabbok River and placed himself between his brother's militia and his family. There, alone and vulnerable, Jacob suddenly found himself wrestling with a stranger. Oddly, Jacob seemed to know that this was a good thing. It didn't take long for him to realize that the stranger was God himself. No doubt Jacob remembered a night 20 years earlier, in a place he named *Beth El* (house of God), when God had promised to bring him safely back some day into the land in which he was born.[118]

The wrestling continued all night until daybreak. When the two exhausted combatants had fought to a standoff, the stranger touched Jacob's hip, wrenching it out of joint and crippling Jacob for life. Still, Jacob persisted, boldly telling the man he would not let him go until the man had given him a blessing.

The stranger finally relented. Jacob then received the blessing he had demanded. It included a new name,

Israel, which means *"one who wrestles with God."* Jacob's offspring would come to be known as the people of Israel—a nation of people who struggle with God.

By virtue of our faith, not in an ethnic or racial sense, you and I can lay claim to the name God originally gave to Jacob and his offspring. We too are the *people who struggle with God.* And this wrestling-with-God identity is another power tool in the peacemaker's arsenal of weapons for combating the personal conflict that invades our lives. Whether we find ourselves turning to the Lord to lift us up when we are about to go to war or calling out to him in the night because the pain of a broken relationship is too great to bear, the Lord wants us to wrestle with him.

Actually, God comes to us, lovingly drawing us into these divine wrestling matches, as he did with Jacob, so he can give us blessings. He wants us to hold him to his promises. He wants us to be persistent in coming to him for every blessing. He wants to uphold us through every conflict life brings our way. Our relationship with our heavenly Father is not a distant one. It is as personal and close as a wrestling match.

Hands Uplifted

This *wrestling-with-God* event has a name. We call it prayer. In prayer we have the penultimate in communication platforms: intimate, personal, direct, immediate, and profoundly effective. And it is exclusively designed for our use. Only the members of God's household have access to this powerful tool.

God gives us this precious tool for our benefit. How easily we become confused about that! We foolishly think God needs our prayers in order to know what is going on in our lives. He doesn't. God knows what we need long before we ask. But he wants us to ask anyway. He wants us to know our help always comes from him. He wants us to remember that it is impossible for us to live apart from him.

The wonder of prayer is that God always actively responds. He listens, and he answers our needs. The hymn verse says it well:

> Oh, what peace we often forfeit,
> Oh, what needless pain we bear,
> All because we do not carry
> Ev'rything to God in prayer![119]

The power tool of prayer is an especially practical tool God has given to his peacemakers. Many of us spend our lives looking for something to do. In his goodness, it sometimes seems as though God has done it all and has taken away from us all the initiative to be agents of change. Prayer is God's answer to that need. Prayer gets things done. It brings about change. It is the tool of choice for people who are called to make a difference. It is a bold, uncompromising tool connected to the kind of faith a child has in a loving parent.[120] If you have been waiting patiently to find something you can do to bring peace and unity to your personal relationships, here it is. In peacemaking, prayer is a game changer.

The Bible tells us, "*Nothing* is impossible with God" (Luke 1:37). That is a very powerful statement. It asserts an absolute. Consider how exclusive a word like *nothing* actually is. You and I know our own limitations. All the impossibilities for us are entirely possible for God. No exceptions! We are talking here about a kind of power the human mind is not really capable of grasping. We can only trust that it is so because God has told us it is so. He is in control of all things—wind and waves, light and darkness.[121] He rules with absolute authority and divine power. And, with the tool of prayer, all of his powerful resources are made available to the peacemakers in his army of believers. Think of the power you have at your disposal—power you can use to address the conflicts in your life and in the lives of others.

The Bible tells us that Jesus often went off by himself to pray. In human flesh, he desperately needed his Father's strength and comfort. He prayed because he was experiencing the kinds of stresses and conflicts in his life we experience in ours—and more.

With the power tool of prayer we can overcome a whole host of demons. Redeemed in the blood of the Lamb, we have the confidence he will answer every prayer. His promise is to give us what we ask for—or something even better.

The Power of Baptism

It is too easy to forget that all things come from God, especially when personal conflict is weighing heavy on one's heart. Conflict has a way of exposing our weaknesses.[122] When we are exposed, our first instinct is to *get decent* before the eyes of both God and others. The apostle Paul connected this natural fear of exposure to our baptisms. He wrote, "All of you who were baptized into Christ have clothed yourselves with Christ" (Galatians 3:27). Paul saw God providing the screen of Christ's absolute righteousness to cover our naked guilt. To use Paul's metaphor, we are *clothed in Christ;* we stand before God covered by Jesus'

We tend to forget that Baptism also gives us the power to live as God's people in the here and now.

holy goodness. That is a very good thing to know—not only for peace of mind but for the peace we need for hearts that occasionally still want to go to war with a neighbor. That incredible spiritual gift is ours through God's gift of Baptism. In our baptisms we are assured of God's forgiveness and the promise that he will let us into his eternal home because we have been washed clean by the Savior's blood.

With all the spiritual blessings that Baptism gives to God's people, we tend to forget that Baptism also gives us the power to live in the here and now as God's people. Luther wrote, "What a great excellent thing baptism is, which delivers us from the jaws of the devil and makes us God's own, suppresses and takes away sin, and then daily strengthens the New Man. . . . For this reason let everyone esteem his baptism as a daily dress in which he is to walk constantly."[123]

If the fear of public exposure as a fool or a patsy is keeping you from reconciling with a brother or sister, remember your baptism. It empowers you to put your fears aside. It strengthens you for the fight between the old Adam and your new man. It moves you to repent of your sins and live a life of obedience to your Savior-God. It empowers you to work toward mending a broken relationship and turns your heart warm to even your worst enemies. Your baptism empowers you to be humbled by your sins and to say to someone you have wronged, "I'm sorry. Please forgive me."

For Thought and Discussion

- Agree or Disagree: God forbids one Christian from taking another Christian to court.

- Why is it so important for peacemakers to be able to know when to base their message on God's law and when it should be a gospel-based message of forgiveness and reconciliation?

- What aspects of conflict may inhibit us from making use of the gift of prayer? How can we overcome this inhibition?

CHAPTER 12

Talkin' Strategy

By Easter the conflict at Peace Lutheran Church was in full bloom. Stan Moralis made good on his threat to have Mark Eastman removed from the Christian Education Committee. He complained that Mark had smeared Pastor Teschendorf's reputation by questioning his work ethic and his ability to effectively carry out his pastoral duties. Mark was not present at the meeting. Tim Teschendorf was. No one spoke in Mark's defense. The elders decided to quietly ask Mark to step down.

Mark refused. In retaliation he hurriedly penned an angry letter addressed to the congregation. In it he condemned Stan for his unloving attitude and called on the Board of Elders to repent for secretly manipulating the church's ministry programs.

The breach between Jill Spiriak and Emily Moralis spread to their daughters. Melanie Moralis and Carolyn Spiriak had once been *BFFs* (best friends forever). Now the girls treated each other with the same disdain their parents held for one another. It didn't take long for Melanie to gather one group of girls to herself and Carolyn to form another clique from her closest friends. The two camps delighted in attacking the opposing group with sarcastic remarks and caustic rumors. The climate at Peace Lutheran School soured almost overnight.

In frustration, four school families met privately with Principal Steve Spiriak to express their concern about the division not only in the school but also within the congregation. Following Steve's recommendation, they quietly drafted a letter to top leaders of their denomination, seeking advice. In the letter their remarks about their pastor's leadership style were quite negative. Their plea was for help. But it was laced with an implied threat to leave Peace Lutheran Church if nothing were done.

Pastor Teschendorf was livid when he heard about the letter. (*How dare they do such a thing without first sharing their concerns with me!*) The following Sunday he preached on a section of Matthew chapter 18—the part that begins with the words, "If your brother sins against you, . . ."[124] After that, the relationship between Pastor Tim and these families became so cold that family members began leaving worship services by a side door to avoid the awkwardness of refusing to shake hands with their own pastor.

Mary Ellen Grovner filed for a divorce. Her lawyer convinced her to pursue a *scorched-earth* settlement. She and Burt had separated shortly after Christmas. A handful of people in the congregation knew about their situation, as did the pastor. But the problems at church consumed most of the church's energy and vitality. The Board of Elders never got around to discussing the Grovner's divorce, and the two seemed to have given up on the counseling sessions. No one noticed when neither Burt nor Mary Ellen were coming to church or attending the Lord's Table.

Burt was deeply distressed over his failed marriage and openly expressed outrage over the financial claims Mary Ellen filed with the court-appointed mediator. When Burt learned that Mary Ellen was dating another man, he was distraught. It hurt that no one from the church bothered to call to ask if he was okay, not even Pastor Teschendorf.

Ned Constantino gave the turmoil a lot of thought as he tossed in bed each night. He prayed that God would help him lead the congregation out of this mess. And through the weeks that followed, Ned was able to put some of his thoughts on paper. At the May meeting of the church council, he came prepared.

When everyone had settled in, Ned asked if he could lead the devotion. Pastor Teschendorf agreed. Ned began by reading Luke 14:25-30:

> Large crowds were traveling with Jesus, and turning to them he said: "If anyone comes to me and does not hate his father and mother, his wife and children, his brothers and sisters—yes, even his own life—he cannot be my disciple. And anyone who does not carry his cross and follow me cannot be my disciple.
>
> "Suppose one of you wants to build a tower. Will he not first sit down and estimate the cost to see if he has enough money to complete it? For if he lays the foundation and is not able to finish it, everyone who sees it will ridicule him, saying, 'This fellow began to build and was not able to finish.'"

Ned continued reading from a prepared script. "*Hate* is a shocking word," he began. "Sometimes it seems as though everyone hates everyone else here at Peace Lutheran Church, and not in the same sense that Jesus had in mind when he said these words. If we are honest, we will admit there is hatred here in this room tonight. Jesus' point was that if we belong to his family, nothing can be allowed to come before him or ahead of him.[125] We've let a lot of things come ahead of Jesus lately—

personal things: pride, anger, envy, gossip, unloving thoughts, mean-spirited actions, character assassination, mistrust. Yes, even hatred. We've each only been interested in getting our own way. If that means hurting somebody else, tough! That's been our attitude.

"It's time to start counting the cost of our conflict. We can't go on pretending to be God's people when our hearts are filled with rancor. That's *hypocrisy!*

"Forgive me for being crass, but the financial cost alone is killing us." Ned stepped to the whiteboard and wrote some numbers. "If an average family gives $2,000 per year and we lose ten families due to our conflict, the financial cost is $20,000 per year. If, God forbid, the conflict continues for a number of years, we pay that cost for every year that we allow it to continue. We've lost more than ten families in the last year. Some of them contributed a lot more than $2,000 a year. And what about the projected financial losses that occur when prospects decide not to become members because of our conflict? Or are we so naïve as to think that visitors won't sense strife in the air and move on to the next church on their list?

"That's the money side. How can we ever begin to measure the spiritual cost? Isn't that why we're here . . . to do ministry?[126] So tell me, what is the cost of doing nothing? If we don't try to make a correction, we'll lose our whole ministry. And that, my dear friends, will put souls in peril."

What Are We Doing Here?

Ned's question about why we are here is pivotal to our understanding of how to address the conflicts that inhibit God's work among us. It's important for anyone caught up in a family argument, a dispute at work, or a tiff with a neighbor to know the answer to that question. The question forces us to decide if we are here to build and strengthen our relationships with one another or destroy them. Those are the only two directions any relationship can go. The sanctified choice is ours. Opting for the God-pleasing option will take us down the road of building and strengthening relationships. Of course, our sinful old Adam would prefer to have things go in the other direction.

Once that choice is clear and the Holy Spirit has moved our new-man hearts to act, a second choice will need to be made. This one has to do with the approach we take toward building our relationships. One option presents the question, *Am I going to work toward helping things go right for others and building them up for the storms of life?* The other asks, *Am I going to help others deal with the things that are going wrong in their lives?*

Both of these alternatives fall under the general heading of *ministry*. The first could be described as a *proactive* approach.[127] The second represents a ministry style that is more *reactive*.[128] Both require a humble servant's attitude. Both are powerful and effective because they are rooted in God's Word. When Christians are busy applying either of these ministry approaches to their relationship-building practices, God blesses the effort.

We need to remember that neither is more important than the other. Unfortunately, we spend most of our time and energy reacting to things that are going wrong when we should be spending more of our time proactively helping things go right. Proactive work should consume more of our resources. (See image on p. 128.) We need to become stronger to prepare for the challenges to our faith life that are sure to come.

But proactive work can also become a rut. If we fail to grasp the distinction between these approaches, we could make the same mistake that the members of Peace are making as they continue to focus on proactive ministry when this is clearly a time to react and seek God's intervention.

At the proactive level, ministry prepares people for life with the faith-strengthening power of God's Word.[129] Ministry in the reactive mode intervenes in spiritual paralysis with the same powerful Word of God.[130]

Proactive work generally involves several interlocking kinds of activity: *listening* with the goal of getting to know people, working at *building stronger relationships, teaching* one another to apply the Bible's truth to everyday life, and *coming together to celebrate* God's promises to us and be encouraged in those promises.

THE PEACEMAKING PYRAMID

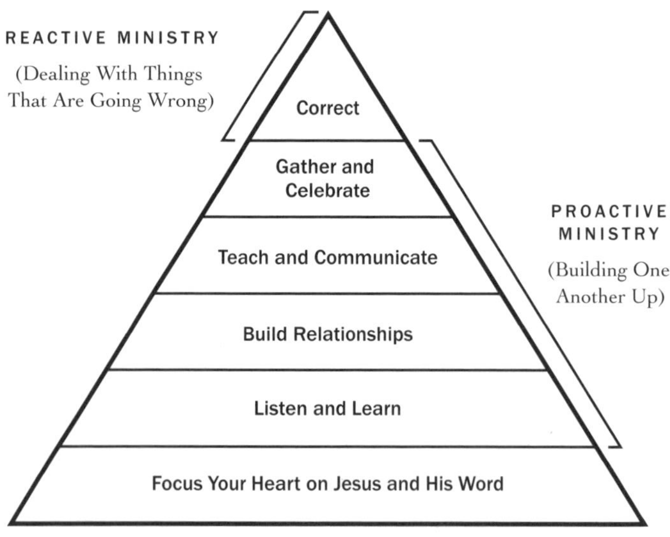

Reactive ministry more often focuses on a single activity. We have been describing this as *intervention.* It addresses a critical threat to someone's faith until it is resolved. The reactive ministry mode zeroes in on correcting a dangerous course that a brother or sister has been caught up in. Sin could be directly involved; or the impasse could be caused by circumstances such as illness and poverty or the hardships connected with personal conflict.

Proactive ministry efforts are able to reach out to larger populations with law and gospel. Reactive ministry is often limited to a one-on-one dynamic. When sin is involved and the sinner is unrepentant, love drives us to minister to one another's needs with a forceful application of God's law. Even when sin is not directly involved, the reactive mode aims at providing comfort and aid to someone in dire need.

Proactive ministry emphasizes an eschatological future. Reactive ministry focuses on a temporal pathology that has spiritual implications. Reactive work, therefore, needs to view the long-term future through the lens of short-term solutions for dealing with a personal obstacle to faith.[131]

Because of conflict's symbiotic relationship with temptation and sin, the role of a peacemaker tends to operate in the reactive mode. Nevertheless, there is also plenty of peacemaking work that needs to be done from a proactive posture as well.

A Strategic Plan to Address Sin

The kind of conflict intervention we are considering here is messy business. Sin is usually the culprit that makes it so messy. Long ago in the world's history, life on our planet became so messy that God had to curtail violence and selfish brutality with a violent intervention of his own.[132]

In the fury of the great deluge, we see God's wrath in action. But in the ark we can also see a gracious God, making a fresh, new start with Noah and his family. Through them his promise of sending a Savior was kept intact.[133]

It was for an imperfect world that our Lord Jesus laid out an intervention strategy for dealing with an erring brother or sister who stubbornly refuses to be held accountable for abusing our trust or attacking our person.[134]

Jesus laid out an intervention strategy to deal with an erring brother or sister who refuses to be held accountable for abusing our trust or attacking our person.

The Lord's strategic plan was recorded in the same chapter of the Bible as the familiar parable about a shepherd who left a flock of 99 to go after one stray sheep.[135] In fact, that parable of the lost sheep and Jesus' intervention strategy are closely connected. His plan is to throw a lifeline to the lost sheep.

> If your brother sins against you, go and show him his fault, just between the two of you. If he listens to you, you have won your brother over. But if he will not listen, take one or two others along, so that "every matter may be established by the testimony of two or three witnesses." If he refuses to listen to them, tell it to the church; and if he refuses to listen even to the church, treat him as you would a pagan or a tax collector. (Matthew 18:15-17)

The Good Shepherd wants us to be like him when we confront a straying brother or sister with an ongoing pattern of sin. Our objective is to move the sinner to repent. He wants us to be gentle and discrete about it.[136] Protect the individual's reputation. Follow *due process*. Let compassion govern your conversation.[137] Go out of your way to demonstrate that you respect the Eighth Commandment. Honor the person's right to confidentiality. Listen patiently. Probe for truth. Weigh evidence.

At the same time, Jesus is brutally honest about those who say they belong to his family but deny their confession by refusing to repent. If the individual remains entrenched in sin, even after you've brought witnesses and shared your concern with the other members of the church, then treat him or her as an unbeliever. Those are words of judgment. In the verses that follow, it becomes clear that when it comes to the well-being of Christ's body of believers, Christians do occasionally have to exercise wise judgment.[138]

But the expression Jesus used to describe an unbeliever here is significant. Instead of saying *unbelievers*, he used the Greek words for pagans and tax collectors—scum of the earth. We must remember that Jesus did some of his most important work among pagans[139] and tax collectors.[140] He loved them. He was eager to become a part of their lives, to make time for them, talk with them, live among them—and die for them. Pagans and tax collectors mattered to Jesus, as do all lost sheep. They are in need of saving.

When conflict threatens, people who are eager to gain the high moral ground have a tendency to misuse this text. Their strategy is to divert attention from their own sins by pointing an accusing finger at an enemy's failure to follow Jesus' prescribed steps. Their self-serving interpretation makes a legalist out of Jesus and a new commandment out of these words of Jesus. Such an accusation is not borne out of humility and concern for a fellow Christian but instead flows from a spirit of sinful pride. When Scripture is abused in this way, the web of conflict becomes even more deadly.

Getting Into Focus

The Holy Spirit made sure that Ned's devotion hit its target. The council members went home that warm May night with Ned's question still ringing in their ears. During the next few weeks, Ned had many opportunities to talk with each of them individually.

At the June meeting, several thoughtful proposals came forward, all aimed at ending the conflict. The discussion was carried on with dignity, even when there were sharp differences regarding the approach to take. The discussion was a breath of fresh air.

Though nothing was actually resolved, the positive atmosphere was a noticeable improvement over previous meetings. With a handful of opposing votes, the council decided to seek professional help from outside. Money was set aside. Then they prayed, asking God to bless the decision that had just been made.

During the next few weeks, there was a flurry of activity centered around finding the right outsider to lead the intervention effort. The individual they sought needed to be an impartial Christian with experience and training. Everyone understood that whomever was selected might also want to enlist the help of other impartial observers.[141]

The church's officers, including Stan Moralis, signed a legally binding contract, stating that they represented a congregation of Christians who "believe that the Bible commands them to make every effort to live at peace and resolve disputes with each other in private or within the Christian community."[142]

The congregation's search quickly led to William Henderson, a man highly recommended by denominational leaders. He was a tall drink of water with a winning smile and a sense of humor that could bring grown men to tears.

At his first meeting with the church council, Mr. Henderson invited everyone to call him *Bill.* Then he laid out some simple ground rules that would make their partnership work efficiently.

It was immediately clear that Bill knew what he was doing and was supremely confident the Lord would bless his work at Peace Lutheran Church. It was also apparent he knew his Bible and wasn't afraid to use it. Everyone was impressed with the emphasis he placed on basing the entire intervention plan on biblical principles. And to make the point stick, he insisted they begin their work right away, with a short Bible study. Intensive study of Scripture would continue with the rest of the congregation over the next few weeks. This is the hallmark of Christ-centered intervention.

Mr. Henderson (Bill) later met with Ned Constantino, who had agreed to serve as the congregation's liaison. Bill explained that he was in the habit of choosing one trusted individual from within the congregation to serve as his own spiritual advisor. They would laugh together, shed tears together, read Scripture together, and pray together. He also noted that the next few months would not be easy and things would almost never go as planned. There would be heartache and disappointment along the way. There would also be much joy in knowing that healing was under way.[143] Bill said it was important for him to have one member who could always be informed about some of the sensitive information that might come up and with whom he could debate the difficult strategic decisions that would have to be made. They would get to know each other well over the next few months.

Bill Henderson also explained that he needed Ned's help in finding a few spiritually mature men and women in the congregation who would have influence within the congregation. "They have to be committed to finding a loving and peaceful solution to your church's problems," said Bill. "And we'll first want to do some relationship building within this little core group. A few couples—good leaders—would be quite helpful. The group would be unofficial, not a part of the church's structure. A few people just quietly meeting for a few weeks around Scripture, strengthening one another in the Word, and thinking through what it would mean to have a congregation in which the people truly loved one another and worked hard to maintain a strong sense of peace and unity. We'll want to get this group started right away."[144]

Finally, Bill explained to Ned that his very first objective would be to get the congregation to change its focus from the kind of bunker mentality that now prevailed to an outlook which fixed everyone's attention on Jesus and his Great Commission.[145] Together, with their hand-selected leadership core, they would hammer out a plan to keep that message before the members of Peace while some other important work was being done to address the personal issues and broken relationships that would require a little more time.

As Ned went home that night, he thanked God for sending a person of Bill Henderson's character and experience.[146] Then he enjoyed the best night's sleep he'd had in months.

For Thought and Discussion

- How may a better understanding of *proactive* and *reactive ministry* improve both types of ministry?

- What is the connection between the parable of the lost sheep and the plan that Jesus proposed as an intervention strategy when a brother or sister has sinned?

- In positive terms, this chapter describes a congregation's decision to seek help from a professional interventionist from outside the congregation to restore peace and unity. This strategy is one of many approaches. What positives/negatives can you see in Bill Henderson's approach?

CHAPTER 13

The Most Excellent Way

Two other people were added to Bill Henderson's intervention team. One was a pastor from a neighboring state; the other, a layperson with skills in communication, counseling, and personal coaching. The three had worked together before. They immediately began to conduct personal interviews with members. These brief one-on-one conversations provided an understanding of the congregation's dynamic makeup. The team members always took a moment to explain that these talks would be kept confidential. The conferences gave the team an opportunity to stress the importance of studying God's Word together. To model this, they began each interview with a five-minute Bible study and a short prayer. Then they carefully explained that their purpose was not to gather evidence, lay blame, or expose sin. (A time might come when sin would have to be addressed, but this was not the time for that.)

Ned Constantino developed a list of ten respected individuals—men and women who had not been drawn into the conflict and were not currently holding church offices or serving on any committees. Ned and Bill narrowed the list to the names of seven strong people. Within a week the group was beginning its work, which initially consisted of studying Scripture. Bill led the sessions.

The group's members quickly grew in confidence. They began to appreciate the gifts each brought to the table. At the same time, they recognized that their congregation was in crisis and needed leadership. The conflicts had to be addressed. As they began to wrestle with the issues and events of the last year, Bill Henderson led them into a study of 1 Corinthians chapter 13—a section of Scripture the apostle Paul had written to a conflict-ridden congregation in Corinth.

> Now I will show you the most excellent way.
>
> If I speak in the tongues of men and of angels, but have not love, I am only a resounding gong or a clanging cymbal. If I have the gift of prophecy and can fathom all mysteries and all knowledge, and if I have a faith that can move mountains, but have not love, I am nothing. If I give all I possess to the poor and surrender my body to the flames, but have not love, I gain nothing.
>
> Love is patient, love is kind. It does not envy, it does not boast, it is not proud. It is not rude, it is not self-seeking, it is not easily angered, it keeps no record of wrongs. Love does not delight in evil but rejoices with the truth. It always protects, always trusts, always hopes, always perseveres.
>
> Love never fails. But where there are prophecies, they will cease; where there are tongues, they will be stilled; where there is knowledge, it will pass away. For we know in part and we prophesy in part, but when perfection comes, the imperfect disappears. When I was a child, I talked like a child, I thought like a child, I reasoned like a child. When I became a man, I put childish ways behind me. Now we see but a poor reflection as in a mirror; then we shall see face to face. Now I

> know in part; then I shall know fully, even as I am fully known.
>
> And now these three remain: faith, hope and love. But the greatest of these is love.

Paul was, of course, basing his thoughts on the most excellent love God has shown to his fallen creatures—a love that is pure, active, selfless, responsive, and utterly boundless. But the passage penetrated the hearts of the group's members, forcing them to think about themselves and their fellow members. They began to see the mistrust, anger, impatience, petty jealousies, lies, self-centered arrogance, unforgiving attitudes, *my-way-or-the-highway* stubbornness, acerbic words, and loveless behaviors that had boiled up as part of their church's culture. In the light of that text, they were able to see selfless *agape* love as God's antidote to the hatred and self-serving motives that gave rise to all their conflict. Yes, they saw God's wondrous and unexpected love stretched out on a cross for each one of them. But now they also saw that same love as the driving mechanism for the congregation's recovery process.[147] They began to understand that if things were going to improve at Peace Lutheran Church, each member would need to become more like Christ. His influence in their lives would have to increase and self would have to decrease.[148]

One member of the group wondered out loud if they should consider "The Most Excellent Way" as a theme and use 1 Corinthians chapter 13 as the cornerstone for the congregation's Bible study. Bill Henderson thought it was a fine idea and said he would begin to work with the concept right away.

The group also talked about repentance, confession, and absolution. They learned how God had sent the prophet Nathan to intervene in David's life.[149] They read

Psalm 51 — David's great expression of personal contrition. They discussed the importance of being reassured of God's forgiveness when our faith has been shaken.[150]

The group agreed there was enough blame to go around.[151] Some of them considered times when they should have spoken up or when they might have been more discrete, loving, patient, or kind. A call for repentance and an opportunity to be reminded of God's full and free forgiveness seemed natural parts of the healing process.

One senior in the group recalled a time perhaps 30 or 40 years ago when members would go regularly to the pastor's office to *announce* their intentions to receive Communion. Everyone was invited to use the opportunity to privately confess a sin that was weighing heavily on his or her heart.[152] The leadership group discussed ways to apply this old practice to their congregation's current divisions.

Bill and his team also spent some time working with the church's leaders. The first sessions were tense. Wounds were deep, and the scars left by the congregation's secret little wars were ugly. There seemed to be little hope for reconciliation between a few of those whose faith lives had been severely damaged by the disputes.

Mark Eastman understood that Jesus wants us to forgive one another. But he had trouble applying the idea to his deeply troubled relationship with Stan Moralis. Mark wondered aloud how many times he would have to put up with Stan's vengeful assaults on his character. He kept saying, "Stan's the one who has to change."

Steve Spiriak still had a problem with Pastor Teschendorf's relentless stranglehold on the church's programs and on the called workers who ran them. Steve explained he was a team player and was more than willing to step forward and tell Pastor Teschendorf that he was sorry for his part in the conflict and that he was willing to forgive Pastor Teschendorf for his role. But Steve could not imagine himself or his colleagues trusting that Pastor Tim would not backslide into old habits. It would be hard to forget the sense of betrayal he and the other faculty members felt.

Tim Teschendorf was filled with remorse for his part in the trouble. He knew he could be demanding. He recognized there were situations in which he seemed to be manipulative. He was ready to go before the congregation to confess his weaknesses.

But Tim privately confided to the intervention team that the joy of his work at Peace had been diluted by constant bickering. He wasn't so sure genuine peace could be restored, at least not under his leadership. He promised to try to do his best to continue to serve Peace because that was what God had called him to do. And he promised to work hard at overcoming his insecurity and to stop micromanaging the church's programs. But the wars of the last few years had taken their toll. He was hoping to get a fresh start somewhere else.

Riders Attached to Forgiveness

The perfect intervention strategy does not exist. We can expect failures, setbacks, and disappointments, even as Jesus did.[153] Sometimes the intervention takes more time than we first anticipated. The fact that a few individuals are unable to see their way toward reconciliation should not surprise us. When someone has hurt us deeply, forgiveness does not come easily, even when we know it is the heavenly Father's will.

When someone has hurt you deeply, forgiveness does not come easily.

It isn't uncommon for people who are trying to find their way out of conflict to consider occupying the turf that lies somewhere in between all-out war and full reconciliation. This is an *almost* offer of forgiveness, but not quite. It can sound something like this: "I'll forgive you, *but* . . ." or "You're forgiven, *as long as* . . ."

Do you recognize a condition being attached? It places the burden of responsibility on someone else. It is forgiveness with a rider attached. And the rider is a backdoor attempt to gain leverage and secure a more advantageous position. The war isn't over. It only looks that way. The appearance that peace has been restored is little more than a charade.

One of the riders we frequently attach to our forgiveness sets limits on the number of times that we have to put up with another person's assaults. The apostle Peter once asked Jesus where the ceiling on our forgiveness should be placed. "Lord, how many times shall I forgive my brother when he sins against me? Up to seven times?" (Matthew 18:21,22). It is this same question that was troubling Mark Eastman.

Jesus' response was straightforward: "Not seven times, but seventy-seven times." Jesus' point was that there is no limit to the number of times we are to forgive. His answer is consistent with his Father's limitless forgiveness policy toward us.[154] How often have you and I appeared before the Father's throne, seeking forgiveness for a sin we have committed again and again?

Another rider some of us try to attach to our forgiveness is a left-handed kind of forgiveness that is first given, then taken back. "I'll forgive you, but I won't ever forget what you've done to me." It's a scorecard approach to forgiveness. The tactic is an attempt to reserve your right to withdraw forgiveness if the offender ever offends you again.

Steve Spiriak was struggling with this temptation. He was not sure yet if he just didn't trust Pastor Teschendorf or if he preferred to have an extra pound of flesh as payback for all the trouble he had been through. It is one thing to be wary in order to protect yourself and your family. It is another thing to keep sins dangling over someone's head like a sword of Damocles so that you can manipulate the individual.

A peacemaker will remind others that real forgiveness is completely unconditional. Of course, only God knows what is going on in hearts. But we can encourage those who are caught up in conflict to do some serious soul-searching to find out if their expressions of forgiveness are genuine and unconditional or just a hedge bet that will pay off later when they are working the system for added leverage.[155]

Your decision to forgive someone who has offended you is an exercise of your sanctified will. When you invite God to be a part of the soul-searching process, let him take you to the foot of the cross to consider what he had to do to free you from the curse of your own sin.[156] With a grateful heart, make your choice to forgive others as Christ forgave you.

Joints From Marrow

The Bible studies, both at the core group's level and within the congregation, had a profound effect on many of the members. The little leadership group was very active in helping to keep the congregation's Bible study moving forward. When members missed a session, these leaders called to gently remind the absentees of the importance these Bible studies had for the church's future direction. Members quickly caught on; attendance was generally excellent.

In one of the earlier sessions for the whole congregation, a young man, who had resigned from a church office a few months earlier in frustration, described the worst months of the conflict as *a suffocating darkness that seemed to never end.* "When the church is coming unglued," he asked, "where can you go to find peace?" For this young man, the whole world appeared to be crashing down as he watched his church being dismantled from the inside. He had become convinced that he was living in the end times.[157] Some nodded in agreement, consciously aware of a similar affectation.

"God cannot give us happiness and peace apart from himself, because it is not there. There is no such thing."[158] The Bible studies began to change that. While the questions remained regarding the school and the budget and the future of the child care center, a new sense of hope was beginning to drift into the members' conversations. One by one each individual was arriving at the same wonderful conclusion: Peace in our church relationships and private lives can only come from God and his love.

One elderly woman said she was shocked to learn that her church was struggling so mightily with, what she called, "such a *big hullabaloo.*" The Bible study had served as a welcome reminder that God's Word always does its job. She stood, strong and tall, and with a voice that rang out loud and clear, she read the words of Hebrews 4:12,13:

> The word of God is living and active. Sharper than any double-edged sword, it penetrates even to dividing soul and spirit, joints and marrow; it judges the thoughts and attitudes of the heart. Nothing in all creation is hidden from God's sight. Everything is uncovered and laid bare before the eyes of him to whom we must give account.

A few were moved to make a public confession—some with tears streaming down their cheeks. Others sought a more private way to express their remorse, as well as their hope. The fellowship hall at Peace Lutheran Church seemed to be filling its lungs with oxygen and expanding its empty chest cavity with new life, like Lazarus rising from the dead. At least it felt that way for some.

Bill Henderson said a quiet prayer of thanksgiving as he left by a side door. There was still plenty of work on the horizon.

For Thought and Discussion

- Was Bill Henderson's intervention role that of a *negotiator*, a *mediator*, or an *arbitrator*?

- Which of Bill Henderson's strategies do you like? Are there any you dislike? Explain.

- Paul's lecture on love in 1 Corinthians chapter 13 ends with the words, "Now these three remain: faith, hope and love. But the greatest of these is love." How important is it for all three components to be part of the peacemaking process? Why is love even greater than faith or hope when conflict is the issue?

- How can God's Word offer hope where no hope existed before?

- Why is forgiveness with conditions attached really no forgiveness at all?

CHAPTER 14

A City of Peace

It had been a busy day for Peter and John. The responsibility to prepare for the Passover celebration had fallen to them. Jesus had asked them personally. They had been honored by his request. This would be their little group's last Pesach (Passover) together. Every detail had to be just right. Their tasks involved securing a room, going to the temple to slaughter and dress the Paschal lamb, purchasing bitter herbs and unleavened bread at the Suk, diluting the wine, roasting the mutton, setting the table, and drawing water from the local well for the foot washing.

When we read about the disciples' last supper together, we ponder the Passover portrait of the lamb's blood splashed on the doorframes of Hebrew dwellings. We may even think about the millions of innocent paschal lambs sacrificed over the centuries. The imagery reminds us of the Lamb of God, pouring his lifeblood on the altar of the cross for the sins of all people. But for many of the Jews at Jesus' time, the feast had evolved into a celebration that was as much about fellowship, togetherness, and renewing old acquaintances. During the disciples' trek south from Galilee to Jerusalem, the mood had been a somber mix of anticipation and anxiety. Jesus had indicated he would be leaving them for a while to be with his Father.[159] The idea of being separated from him was a hard concept to process.[160] Furthermore, he seemed more driven than usual—though the mission still remained vague.[161] Along the way, the disciples had joined other pilgrims on the road to Jerusalem. To pass the time and remain focused on their religious objective, the travelers sang familiar psalms to lift their spirits. One psalm in particular described the heartfelt relationships they cherished.

> How good and pleasant it is
>   when brothers live
>   together in unity!
> Like precious oil poured
>   on the head . . .
>   running down on Aaron's beard,
>   down upon the collar of his robes.
> It is as if the dew of Hermon
>   were falling on Mount Zion.
> For there the LORD bestows his blessing,
>   even life forevermore.[162]

The disciples' formal training was coming to an end. In the last three years, they had grown very close to Jesus. Their camaraderie with one another had flourished as well. Soon they would return to their hometowns to teach others what they had learned from their rabbi.

And, oh, how much they had learned! Yet how little they truly understood! Some important issues still remained unsettled. Like the question of *greatness*.[163] How ironic that on a day when the paschal celebration was supposed to be warming hearts with the joy of unity and fellowship, an old dispute resurfaced.[164] Each man, with siblinglike rivalry, clamored for the place of honor at the table.

Jesus patiently explained that greatness was not measured in his kingdom as the world measures it.[165] The lesson had been broached before. But when the time came for washing feet, no one volunteered. Each thought too highly of himself to stoop to such a demeaning task.

Shedding his outer coat and wrapping a towel around his waist, Jesus humbly knelt at the foot of each student and began the foot-washing ritual. He wanted each of them to realize that the desire for elevated status was evidence of an attitude saturated with sinful self-centeredness. He was connecting the idea of *humble service* to their future as the church's leaders—a future that would bring them blessings as they would exercise humility in their relationships with others.[166] "The one who rules," he softly said, "should be the one who serves."[167]

When it was his turn, Peter resisted. He indicated that he would prefer to show reverence for Jesus by washing the Master's feet, and not the other way around.

Jesus used Peter's response to explain a far greater need for spiritual cleansing. "Unless I wash *you,* . . ." said Jesus.

The lesson was no longer about honoring Jesus or personal humility, it was picture language for divine grace and the spiritual bath we so desperately need through the forgiveness of sins. Werner Franzmann writes,

> Our sins make us unclean, filthy in the sight of God. We cannot cleanse ourselves. We can be washed clean only by the atoning blood of Jesus.[168]

Later Jesus would institute a sacrament that, along with the eating and drinking, would assure us with the words "given and poured out for you for the forgiveness of sins."

Peter understood the word picture. If his sin was the issue, he wanted Jesus to wash him from head to toe.

As the evening wore on, Jesus spoke about other relationships—some that would cause great difficulty. "The world hates you," he declared. "If they persecuted me, they will persecute you also. . . . They will treat you this way because of my name, for they do not know the One who sent me. . . . All this I have told you so that you will not go astray. . . . A time is coming when anyone who kills you will think he is offering a service to God. . . . You will remember that I warned you."[169]

The Lord also spoke of his loving relationship with his heavenly Father—of their perfect unity. He described the Godhead's love for his followers.[170] This would be Jesus' final discourse. He would love them all (including Judas) to the end.[171] He wanted to strengthen their faith for the gut-wrenching days that lay ahead. "Remain in me, and I will remain in you," he said.[172] "Bear fruit—fruit that will last."[173] "Love one another. As I have loved you."[174] "The Father himself loves you because you have loved me and have believed that I came from God."[175]

He prayed for his disciples. The privileged work of carrying Jesus' message of redemption and reconciliation with God to the far corners of the planet had been given to them. "Holy Father, protect them by the power of your name . . . so that they may be one as we are one."[176]

Then he prayed for his church—for you and me and for our relationships with one another. He prayed that we may have the same tender relationship with his Father that he knows. He asked for us to have the same beautiful oneness with the Father that he enjoys. "May they be brought to complete unity," he prayed, "to let the world know that you sent me and have loved them even as you have loved me."[177] *Fellowship, unity, oneness, godly relationships*—these were the golden threads woven through the last Passover's conversations.

Years later the apostle Paul would note that the unity Jesus prayed for in the upper room is centered in the *oneness* we have in him.[178] It is a gift that transcends all others—a gift to be cherished, and shared. We are one in Christ Jesus and his enduring Word. Such unity does not come to us on the basis of gender, race, ethnicity, or social status. We will not find it in traditions, history, culture, or even family. Nor should we look for it in the church's programs, its politics, or its leaders. We are one in Christ.[179]

Many Peace Lutheran Church members were finally beginning to rediscover this extraordinary truth.

Celebration Time, C'mon!

As adults were starting to realize that the way out of their congregation's paralyzing conflict would come through forgiveness, some of their children were already beginning to think about the afterglow.

On a warm afternoon in early June, Jill Spiriak was surprised to see her daughter Carolyn strolling up the sidewalk arm-in-arm with Melanie Moralis. Their carefree expressions telegraphed a dramatic change in their hostilities.

Jill intercepted the girls on the patio. "Hey, I thought you two were archenemies?" It was an awkward moment. Jill had not spoken with Melanie for months, though she taught in the same building where Melanie attended school. Prior to the rift, Jill had been able to talk with Melanie like a mother talks with her own daughter. Now it required some effort just to make eye contact. Yet it felt good to see both girls so happy in each other's company. "Did you patch things up?" she asked.

"That's ancient history, Mom."

"I see," observed Jill. Her tone was cool. But she couldn't find it in her heart to begrudge Carolyn the joy of Melanie's friendship. "I'm glad for you both. . . . And when did this miracle cease-fire occur?"

"Oh, it's more than just a cease-fire, Mrs. Spiriak," bubbled Melanie with a smile aimed in Carolyn's direction. "It is a miracle." Melanie's tan face was radiant in the sunlight, and her eyes sparkled. Jill had forgotten how mature Melanie was for her age. "We've been working up to it for a couple of days," volunteered the bright 13-year-old. "This morning we finally sat down and apologized to each other."[180]

"Mom," interrupted Carolyn, "we want to have a party." She could barely contain her enthusiasm. "We want to, you know, . . . *celebrate*." Before Jill could respond, the two were listing ideas that had apparently already been discussed—decorations, the menu, thoughts about whom they might invite, and the wording on the invitation. They were eager to share the thrill of their resurrected friendship with others.

Over the next few days Jill became preoccupied with the idea of trying to find some peace for herself, just as Carolyn and Melanie had. *Out of the mouths of babes,* she thought![181] Only, in her case, it would take a real miracle to make things right with Emily.

When the miracle finally happened, Jill had sat tearfully in her car for an hour about a block from the Moralis' home. She wasn't sure if she could actually do this. She needed more time to build up her courage. Facing her own mistakes in this relationship was the most painful part. How could Emily ever forgive her? Jill felt weak, paralyzed with fear. *What if Emily rejects my apology? What if she disses me outright?* thought Jill. This would take every bit of courage she could muster.[182]

God was with her. Jill knew that. He would provide the resources she needed.[183] During that hour she prayed.[184] She silently repeated the words of Ephesians 4:3: *"Make every effort to keep the unity of the Spirit through the bond of peace."* Jill realized she had not been living up to that standard lately. There was no mistaking the hardened attitude she had been cultivating in her heart toward Emily. That had to change. Never mind the things that Emily had said and done to hurt her! Jill was sure God would make it happen; he would change the condition of her stony heart.[185] She didn't want this to go on another day, or even another hour.

The Sunset Principle

The Bible tells us there is an urgency to resolving disputes. Paul wrote, "In your anger do not sin: Do not let the sun go down while you are still angry, and do not give the devil a foothold" (Ephesians 4:26,27). In other words, deal with it quickly. Today, if possible. In this way, a bad situation won't escalate into something more dangerous. In Matthew 5:23,24 Jesus taught, "If you are offering your gift at the altar and there remember that your brother has something against you, leave your gift there in front of the altar. First go and be reconciled to your brother; then come and offer your gift." A festering grudge is an open invitation to more discord. God sees our conflicts and broken relationships as urgent. He wants us to make conflict resolution our highest priority.

God sees our conflicts as urgent. He wants us to resolve them as early as possible.

We can only be truly joyful regarding God's *shalom* if we are also at peace with one another. So it is important that we address conflicts early, before they can get a head of steam. That truth is magnified many times over in our most personal and intimate relationships. Married couples, for example, would do better in applying the Sunset Principle if husbands and wives established the daily habit of finishing their days together with a prayer that covers some of the disappointments and highlights of the day. When a disagreement threatens to disturb unity and peace, this practice forces a conversation about resolving the matter before retiring. You'd be surprised at how many family altercations can be avoided by joining together in seeking God's help with a potential conflict.

A Meal to Heal

After many months of heartache, Jill was finally ready to tell Emily how sorry she was about the things she had thought, said, and done. Now she wondered if the whole mess might have been avoided if she had dealt with it in the right way at the very beginning. But before she could get out of the car, three light taps on her car window interrupted her thoughts. It was Emily.

The healing began almost immediately as each, in turn, laid her heart bare and asked for forgiveness. Both were surprised at how quickly the burden lifted. Their new freedom was palpable and real.[186] They offered a prayer of thanks together.[187]

The two drove to their favorite restaurant and ordered lunch. The next few hours were a tearful blur of catching up on all the details of life they had once shared in the intimacy of their friendship. Eventually they stumbled on to the delicate questions still facing their conflict-ridden congregation. Those problems were still real and pressing. But the church's concerns no longer seemed insurmountable. The two could actually talk about some of the troublesome things being discussed by other members in the Bible studies. Now both saw the beauty of their daughters' idea to throw a party. Everyone had a reason to celebrate. Maybe there were others who felt the same need.

When Jill and Emily shared their idea for a celebration with Bill Henderson, they discovered that some plans were already in the making. They also learned that God had already provided the necessary components for the kind of party that would serve as a reminder of the spiritual implications of this miracle. It would be a party of the highest order, celebrated around the spiritual supper that Jesus himself instituted on that first Maundy Thursday. All the key elements would be there: food for nurturing their faith, an honored guest's presence,[188] fellowship with God and one another. Peace Lutheran Church would throw a party that would commemorate all the spiritual blessings they enjoyed because of Jesus' saving work.[189] And then they would get on with the work that Jesus had commissioned them to do.[190] That is how Christians celebrate their restoration into God's household of faith.[191] It was the perfect way for these members to give thanks for God's goodness in helping them end their nightmare.[192]

The date for the congregation's celebratory meal was set. Plans were made to make this a special day of thanksgiving. The members of Peace Lutheran Church would come to God's altar with hearts truly reunited to receive the body that had been crushed under the burden of their sins and the blood that had been shed to reconcile them with their loving Father in heaven, and which made it possible for them to reconcile with one another. Their old at-war hearts had been transformed by the gospel into hearts that were once again at peace. They were equipped, and fully committed, to march forward like an army of one, following the Lamb's banner, ready to carry out their church's ministry. But when the day of celebration finally arrived, the joy that members expressed to one another was tainted with a note of deep regret and sadness. Word spread quickly: The Sunday news included a brief story about a former member, Burt Grovner. In the early morning hours, Burt had apparently lost control of his motorcycle and crashed into a concrete bridge abutment. His broken remains were found a short distance from his bike. Burt probably had died instantly.

Some members barely remembered Burt. Those who did recalled that he had not been very regular in his church attendance or at the Lord's Supper. After his bitter divorce, he just seemed to disappear. No one had seen or heard from him since. Too bad! Those who had known Burt agreed that he would have appreciated this special day of celebration. Burt had always been a man of peace. He was only 46. *What a shame!*

The Peace Offering

The e-mail simply said, "Please meet tonight in the church chancel around 7:00 P.M." Stan Moralis recognized the initials T. E. T.: Timothy Eton Teschendorf. *But Tim Teschendorf usually explains things in a lot more detail,* thought Stan. *And why does he want to meet in the chancel?* Stan guessed it had something to do with the ongoing discord at church. He had plenty of doubts about the intervention plan; it still seemed like a bad idea. Six months ago he had agreed to it out of frustration. Could the process now be proving to be a failure? Were folks beginning to see Bill Henderson as a fraud? Was Pastor Teschendorf beginning to feel the same way? As far as Stan was concerned, Henderson's team was sticking its nose into something they didn't understand—a conflict embedded long ago in the church's history and culture. And they were charging a hefty fee.

Stan decided he would go to meet with the pastor. He respected Tim Teschendorf's tenacity, and he held the pastoral office in high regard.[193]

Unlike some of the other members, Stan had not been able to let go of the terrible things that had happened over the last year. When Emily explained how she and Jill found peace and rediscovered the joy of their once-dead friendship, Stan's only thought was that these two women had never been privy to all of the hateful words and mean-spirited infighting that had gone on behind closed doors. All too well he knew the condition of his own heart. His disdain for Mark Eastman (and company) ran about as deep as one man could have for another, even if they were both members of the same church. That's just the way things were. No professional interventionist was going to change it.

Stan entered the church through the narthex. Pastor Teschendorf was sitting in the front pew, waiting for Stan. Or so he thought. When he approached the silhouette, Stan was surprised to find that the pew was not occupied by Tim Teschendorf. It was Mark Eastman instead. Now Stan understood the cryptic nature of Tim's email. Teschendorf had lured him into attending a meeting that would include Mark Eastman. Mark had probably been duped in the same way. Stan was angry. How could Pastor Tim do such a thing? No one knew the contempt these two men held for each other more than Tim Teschendorf.

A few awkward minutes of silence passed. Mark finally broke the silence: "Teschendorf told me he wanted to meet here."

"Me too," said Stan with an icy tone. The air was thick with intolerance and ill will. Neither man could face the other squarely.

On the altar lay a white envelope. Stan noticed it first. It was addressed to Stan and Mark. "I have a feeling the good pastor isn't going to show," mumbled Stan, indicating that the envelope could hold an explanation. Stan read it to himself; then he handed it to Mark. It read:

> Dear Stan and Mark,
> Please accept my apologies for the cloak-and-dagger tactic. As you have probably guessed, I won't be joining you. My physical presence would only stir old resentments. However, my thoughts and prayers will be with you as you consider what follows.
> To begin, you both need to know that I have wrestled with my conscience and the sins of pride, arrogance, jealousy, anger, and selfishness that have gotten in the way of my ministry at Peace. I know I am forgiven and that God loves me. But in that knowledge, I am requesting a call into another parish. The change will be good for everyone.
> As it turns out, that decision places me in a better position to be able to give both of you a valuable gift,[194] so please humor me by facing the altar and noting the cross that hangs above it. (Not long ago I stood in the very same spot.) Then ask yourselves this simple question: *Is it finished?*[195] Don't leave until you are both satisfied that you have thoroughly considered the question and have answered it in a way that glorifies God's name.[196] When you know the gift, leave your *peace offerings* there on the altar.[197]

Last one out, please turn off the lights and lock the door.
Shalom,
T. E. T.

For Thought and Discussion

- Why is it so important to regularly celebrate our reconciliation with God and one another? What impact should your answer have on your church's attitude toward the Sacrament of the Altar?

- What makes God's party plan so much better than the ideas people may have?

- What thoughts were going through your mind as you read about Burt's tragic accident?

- What do you think Tim Teschendorf meant when he said he was in a better position to give both men a valuable gift?

- What thoughts may have gone through the minds of these two men as they stood at the foot of the cross contemplating Pastor Teschendorf's question? What scenarios may have played out as a result of their meeting?

- What was the *peace offering* Pastor Teschendorf hoped Mark and Stan would leave on the altar?

PART THREE

The Amalekites

The wisdom that comes from heaven is first of all pure; then peaceloving, considerate, submissive, full of mercy and good fruit, impartial and sincere. Peacemakers who sow in peace raise a harvest of righteousness.

JAMES 3:17,18

CHAPTER 15

Coals of Fire

The distinction between those conflicts that occur among believers and those that occur among believers and unbelievers is an important one. So far our conversation has been generally limited to conflicts among Christians. We've noted that Christian brothers and sisters certainly do disagree (in matters of *adiaphora,* for example, and also with regard to doctrine and practice). But God does not want members of his *church militant* to view one another with hatred, animosity, or hostility.

The foundation for relationships bound together in Christ Jesus is love.[198] The preceding chapters have focused on the premise that our love compels us to correct one another when a pet sin or biblical error threatens the faith life of one of Christ's own.[199] But we have also learned that there is a right way to approach such correction and a wrong way.[200] Now we are going to turn our attention to the relationships we have with those who do not share our faith in Jesus—*unbelievers,* folks who may even curse Jesus' name and despise his followers.

Our faith offends unbelief. You may recall that it was Cain's unbelief that drove him to murder Abel because he was offended. And Jesus warned us not to be surprised when the unbelieving world hates us for trusting in him as our one and only Savior.[201]

Knowing the Real Enemy

After Jesus and his disciples had eaten their last Passover meal together, the Twelve (now down to the Eleven) retreated to the Mount of Olives. Jesus plunged into the night, pressing on toward a secluded garden named *Gethsemane.* Peter, James, and John quietly followed. While the three hunkered into a small hollow to rest, Jesus continued on for a few hundred feet to pray.

Not long after, footfall interrupted the stillness. A torch bobbed in the distance, casting an eerie glow against moving shadows. The three strained to understand the commotion.

Temple guards strode into view. Their spokesman gruffly announced they were seeking Jesus of Nazareth. A familiar figure stepped from their ranks: Judas. He greeted Jesus with a customary kiss.

Peter burned with rage. The Pharisees had been harassing Jesus for weeks. Apparently, they had managed to lure one of the rabbi's own into betraying him. *Is this it?* wondered Peter. *Is this when I put everything on the line?* As his mind reeled, Peter's left hand searched for the hilt of the short sword strapped to his thigh. It slid effortlessly from its leather sheath. Suddenly he was flailing away without considering target or technique.

Malchus, a servant of the high priest, stumbled as he tried to avoid the blade's sweeping arc. Cold steel grazed the right side of his head, severing his ear. Blood leaked down one side of his face.

A calming voice spoke. It was the Master's. "Put your sword away!"[202]

Peter was convinced this fight had come to him. He reacted decisively and with passion. He was willing to die or to take the life of another human being, even if he might be fighting the wrong enemy. It was a foolish choice. A life had almost been needlessly snuffed out because Peter was operating with some wrong assumptions. His most serious error was to assume his primary enemy was human. Such a mistake could be catastrophic.

Peter assumed his primary enemy was human. What a mistake!

For sinners, the ultimate enemy is him who has the power to condemn souls to hell. "I tell you, my friends," said Jesus, "do not be afraid of those who kill the body and after that can do no more. But I will show you whom you should fear: Fear him who, after the killing of the body, has power to throw you into hell. Yes, I tell you, fear him" (Luke 12:4,5).

People living in unbelief should be shaking in their boots. The One who has the power to throw us into hell is God. Someday sinners will have to face their Judge, and the divine Judge will show no mercy to anyone who is not covered in Jesus' righteousness.[203] Oh, yes, our just and righteous God is to be feared!

But not by us.[204] True, at birth you and I were at war with God. We were dead to his loving embrace, blind to the light of his hope. But listen to the apostle Paul's description of God's remarkable grace working through faith to change our hopeless status:

> As for you, you were dead in your transgressions and sins, in which you used to live when you followed the ways of this world and of the ruler of the kingdom of the air, the spirit who is now at work in those who are disobedient. All of us also lived among them at one time, gratifying the cravings of our sinful nature and following its desires

> and thoughts. Like the rest, we were by nature objects of wrath. But because of his great love for us, God, who is rich in mercy, made us alive with Christ even when we were dead in transgressions. . . . For it is by grace you have been saved, through faith—and this not from yourselves, it is the gift of God—not by works, so that no one can boast. (Ephesians 2:1-5,8,9)

Because of Jesus' redeeming work, we are no longer at enmity with God. Our broken relationship with him has been reconciled. God reconciled us to himself. He is our Friend, our loving Father, our Savior, and our heavenly King. That is our eternal reality.

But hold on! The Bible also tells us that while we remain in this life, there still is an enemy who seeks to destroy our eternal future with God. He skulks around, launching sneak attacks on the faithful.[205] This is not just an enemy; he is the enemy—the one against whom God himself swore a holy oath of eternal enmity.[206] This enemy has a name: *Satan.*

Paul was inspired to bluntly identify our soul's deadliest enemy. And then he told us exactly how to prepare for the enemy's inevitable assaults:

> Finally, be strong in the Lord and in his mighty power. Put on the full armor of God so that you can take your stand against the devil's schemes. For our struggle is not against flesh and blood, but against the rulers, against the authorities, against the powers of this dark world and against the spiritual forces of evil in the heavenly realms. Therefore put on the full armor of God, so that when the day of evil comes, you may be able to stand your ground, and after you have done everything,

> to stand. Stand firm then, with the belt of truth buckled around your waist, with the breastplate of righteousness in place, and with your feet fitted with the readiness that comes from the gospel of peace. In addition to all this, take up the shield of faith, with which you can extinguish all the flaming arrows of the evil one. Take the helmet of salvation and the sword of the Spirit, which is the word of God. And pray in the Spirit on all occasions with all kinds of prayers and requests. With this in mind, be alert and always keep on praying for all the saints. (Ephesians 6:10-18)

The devil and his legion of lost angels comprise an alarming enemy force—one that you and I have no chance of standing up to on our own. His army has the potential to bring souls to perdition. He works constantly, tirelessly (and especially hard) at undermining the confidence of God's people.

But to keep us from despairing at the prospect of going head-to-head with Satan and all his evil forces, Paul also expressed his trust in God's promise to protect and defend us from this deadliest of all adversaries.[207] Writing to the congregation in Rome, where many of the saints were facing martyrdom, the apostle affirmed, "I am convinced that neither death nor life, neither angels nor demons, neither the present nor the future, nor any powers, neither height nor depth, nor anything else in all creation, will be able to separate us from the love of God that is in Christ Jesus our Lord" (Romans 8:38,39).[208]

While Satan's attacks are aimed at wreaking spiritual havoc, he has also enlisted the at-war hearts of unbelievers to distract us with physical and emotional conflicts. His strategy is to take our attention away from important spiritual battles by presenting us with lesser skirmishes to keep us occupied. His knows that clashes with our unbelieving neighbors can weaken us and make us vulnerable to his probes at our faith. He is banking that this strategy will eventually lead us to doubt and ultimately unbelief.

The case of Judas Iscariot provides a biblical example of the devil's corrupt plan. A full year before the betrayer actually carried out his treachery, Jesus had already noted that Judas was letting Satan have access to his heart as he nursed the sin of covetousness.[209]

As early as Genesis 3:15 we get the idea that some individuals (like Judas) are so steeped in unbelief they actually relinquish their will to Satan. The Bible identifies such individuals as "Satan's *seed*" (or his *offspring*).

Dealing with folks who have become so hardened to God's loving embrace can be problematic. They will do anything to impede the free flow of the gospel message. They are a threat to God's people. On the surface that threat appears to be attacking us at a physical or emotional level. Truth is, our conflicts with hardened and hate-filled people can also lead to our own spiritual downfall.

Before sending his followers on a particular evangelism mission, Jesus explained that the environment they were entering suggested that they should carry weapons.[210] Perhaps the areas in which they would be evangelizing were already known to be hostile to Jesus' saving message. In any case, the Lord was not using figurative language here; he was speaking about packing deadly weapons (swords) that could be used to defend life and limb. This doesn't sound like the gentle Lord Jesus pictured on the pages of Sunday school books. But his point is well-taken. We have the right to defend ourselves. And there is great wisdom in remaining alert and putting aside one's naiveté.[211]

A Hard Lesson

This talk of weaponry and tactical support leads to our final discussion. We've saved this lesson for last because the concept is just so difficult to buy into. (Had we introduced it earlier, we might have lost some readers.)

To make the point, consider one of the many war narratives in Scripture. This one describes a familiar battle between the people of Israel and the Amalekites (Exodus 17:8-15). It is best known for the word picture of Aaron and Hur faithfully propping up Moses' arms high in the air (like a banner to inspire Israel's army) as Moses pleaded for a victory from God. From the beginning it was clear: This military action was sanctioned by a higher authority.[212] The narrative brings to mind the Fourth Commandment and the Bible's teachings regarding God-given authority.

For our discussion, we are interested in another more subtle inference that can be drawn from this account. The Amalekites were a tribe of warmongers. They lived in the wilderness of the Sinai Desert, making their living by attacking the dawdlers who traveled a mile or two behind the main caravans. These people were often sick or disabled. In most cases they were unable to fend for themselves. As they slowly made their way north, the people of Israel sustained many losses, far too many to continue to ignore these despicable hit-and-run attacks on the weak. The Amalekites had to be destroyed. And God blessed the Israelite warriors with victory—a sweet revenge for all the souls lost to the accursed Amalekite devils!

But the narrative doesn't end there. The Lord had something profound to say about this particular conflict; and Moses echoed God's words.

> Then the LORD said to Moses, "Write this on a scroll as something to be remembered and make sure that Joshua hears it, because I will com-

> pletely blot out the memory of Amalek from under heaven."
>
> Moses built an altar and called it The LORD is my Banner. He said, "For hands were lifted up to the throne of the LORD. The LORD will be at war against the Amalekites from generation to generation." (For the whole story, see Exodus 17:8-15.)

Did you get the point? God wanted Moses to take down some dictation: *Write this down! I want every succeeding generation to remember what I, the Lord your God, am about to declare.* And what was the declaration? As a renegade nation, Amalek would pay the ultimate price: extinction. But, as God was their Judge, even after they had been completely eradicated, their treachery would continue to be remembered in infamy. This was God declaring eternal enmity with Satan's wretched *seed.* From that day on Satan's unbelieving offspring had a new name: *Amalek.*

So, what exactly is the point? When we have been wronged, you and I find it almost impossible to let God be the Judge.[213] We prefer to fight our own battles. And there is a sinful reason behind that preference. Our old Adam is constantly urging us to step into God's role and seek revenge for our own self-gratification. The concept of getting payback is galvanized in our psyche. *If you hit me, I will hit you back.* The threat is often intensified with the suggestion that my retaliatory strike promises to be more severe than my enemy's original blow. We are so conditioned to seeking reprisal that our basic need to retaliate often operates at a visceral level.[214]

Jesus understood this human impulse. The weapon of choice in his example was an open hand. But it might just as well have been a fist, a club, a gun, or a hate-filled remark. Here is what Jesus would have us consider when we are tempted to respond according to our base instinct:

> You have heard that it was said, "Eye for eye, and tooth for tooth." But I tell you, Do not resist an evil person. If someone strikes you on the right cheek, turn to him the other also. And if someone wants to sue you and take your tunic, let him have your cloak as well. If someone forces you to go one mile, go with him two miles. Give to the one who asks you, and do not turn away from the one who wants to borrow from you. . . . I tell you: Love your enemies and pray for those who persecute you. (Matthew 5:38-44)

Someone may argue that Jesus was creating a figurative model when he said this—that he didn't mean we should literally (or willingly) offer the other cheek to our enemy for another shot. Others express concern that Jesus' words could be easily misinterpreted as a license for abuse. They fear sending a message to vulnerable women or children, telling them they must abide abusive husbands or fathers who treat them like human punching bags.

None of these concerns line up squarely with Jesus' intent, although he was, without question, willing to endure such injustice and abuse during his own sojourn among sinners.[215]

To understand the lesson, we have to go only as far as the introduction. The Lord Jesus was talking about getting revenge. The customary payback for an eye plucked out in a hand-to-hand fight was that the aggressor's eye should be poked out as well. A broken tooth could be avenged by breaking the tooth of the person who struck the initial blow.

With perfect clarity, we get Jesus' intended meaning. This is not the way he wants his followers to behave. To serve him, to be the salt of the earth and light of the world, you and I are called to a standard that rises above all others. In fact, passing up the chance to get revenge is to be considered a blessing.[216] Reflect on Paul's encouragement to the Christians at Corinth. His hope was that their behavior would be distinctively different from the world's norms.

> By the meekness and gentleness of Christ, I appeal to you—I, Paul, who am "timid" when face to face with you, but "bold" when away! I beg you that when I come I may not have to be as bold as I expect to be toward some people who think that we live by the standards of this world. For though we live in the world, we do not wage war as the world does. The weapons we fight with are not the weapons of the world. On the contrary, they have divine power to demolish strongholds. We demolish arguments and every pretension that sets itself up against the knowledge of God, and we take captive every thought to make it obedient to Christ. (2 Corinthians 10:1-5)

So why is this teaching so hard? It is not a complex idea. Even a child can grasp it.

It is a hard teaching because it is so difficult to apply. The secular world challenges us to ignore it, even violate it, at every turn: *If somebody smacks you in the face, hit him back.* The harder, the better! It is a way of life. Grab all the leverage, upper hand, clout, dignity, pride, and self-determined justice you can get! Media promotes this ethic. Culture reinforces it. Society refines it. Our vocabulary and lifestyle project it. Most of us are so confused by these two opposing values that we have convinced ourselves that Jesus' teaching is a nice ideal, even though we have already reserved the right to deviate from it when under pressure. That attitude forces us to live with a double standard.

That attitude misses the whole point. Setting one's heart on payback is to doubt God's promise to avenge the deeds of the wicked *for us*.[217] "It is mine to avenge," says Amalek's Judge. That's why God wanted the people of Israel to remember the Amalekites. They were to recall the fate of the tribe of Amalek as a judgment that came directly from God. Even in battle, defending their lives and the lives of their families, the Israelites were to remain dispassionate about the enemy, remembering that it is God who judges and it is God who punishes even the most deplorable, heinous sins.

When we are seeing a fellow human being behaving like the devil incarnate, we need to forget our urge for getting revenge and remember that God says to trust him when he says, "I will repay."[218]

Peter's experiences with conflict taught him some important lessons. Perhaps he was recalling his own impetuous response to treachery when, years later, the man who had brandished a sword in Gethsemane's garden wrote, "Do not repay evil with evil or insult with insult, but with blessing, because to this you were called so that you may inherit a blessing" (1 Peter 3:9). Peter had come the long way around to seeing conflict and peace from God's point of view.

A Bold New Strategy

For sinner-saints like us, pulling off something as simple as walking in Jesus' sandals is never an easy assignment. He is God; we are not. Hanging from a cross, he could pray, "Father, forgive them."[219] In the heat of our battles, we find that kind of prayer a challenge. A good test to determine if you are guilty of hating someone is to ask yourself, *Can I sincerely pray for this person?* If you are forced to admit that you cannot, it's time to do some serious soul-searching.

When it comes to having a meaningful relationship with an unbeliever (particularly one who is hostile to our faith and acts like Satan's offspring), we are way out on a radical limb, living in a counterintuitive no-man's-land where the only worthwhile plan is to trust Jesus at his word. "Fear not; I am with you," he whispers. "Now go and do your work. Remember, you were once in the same boat. Love those unbelievers, even as I have loved you. Reach out to them with my peace."[220]

You and I have a purpose and a meaning for our lives that line up with the commission that our Lord has given us. Like the old hymn says:

Onward, Christian soldiers, Marching as to war,
With the cross of Jesus Going on before.
Christ, the royal master, Leads against the foe;
Forward into battle See his banners go!
Onward, Christian soldiers, Marching as to war,
With the cross of Jesus Going on before.

Like a mighty army Moves the Church of God;
Brothers, we are treading Where the saints have trod.
We are not divided, All one body we,
One in hope and doctrine, One in charity.
Onward, Christian soldiers, Marching as to war,
With the cross of Jesus Going on before.

Crowns and thorns may perish, Kingdoms rise and wane,
But the Church of Jesus Constant will remain.
Gates of hell can never 'Gainst that Church prevail;
We have Christ's own promise, And that cannot fail.
Onward, Christian soldiers, Marching as to war,
With the cross of Jesus Going on before.

Onward, then, ye faithful; Join the happy throng,
Blend with ours your voices In the triumph song:
Glory, laud, and honor Unto Christ the King;
This through countless ages Saints and angels sing.

Onward, Christian soldiers, Marching as to war,
With the cross of Jesus Going on before.

(CW 537:1-4)

Christianity is not for the faint of heart. But, then, the new heart that God's love has implanted within us is anything but fainting. It's a vibrant heart—one that can, and does, "bless those who persecute [us]." Did you hear that? "Bless and do *not curse.*"[221] Our at-peace heart is eager to do its very best "to live in peace with all men."[222]

The relationships we have with the unbelieving world explain why we are still here. We have work to do. The nature of some of our work could take us out of our comfort zones and place us into hostile territory. Our approach to seeking out our target is radically different from the approach that the unbelieving world would take. The Lord points the way: "If your enemy is hungry, give him food to eat; if he is thirsty, give him water to drink. In doing this, you will heap burning coals on his head, and the LORD will reward you" (Proverbs 25:21,22).

The Next Level

Strategic plans come in all shapes and sizes and with varying degrees of complexity. Some work better than others. For wisdom and simplicity, the strategy Jesus outlined as a first-blush door opener for sharing the gospel with our unbelieving neighbors is a concept every peacemaker needs to consider. It seems like a good way to give closure to our conversations as we challenge one another to reach for the next level, which is to have meaningful relationships with those who may still consider us the enemy. To his followers (including you and me), Jesus once suggested, "When you enter a house, first say, '[Shalom] to this house.'"[223] The *shalom* you and

I have to share with a world that is still at war with its Creator is the eternal peace of God's unearned forgiveness and undeserved love. Go in peace. Go with God's peace in hand, and live the life of a peacemaker.

For Thought and Discussion

- Why is it important to make a distinction between conflicts that occur within the community of Christians and conflicts that occur between Christians and unbelievers?

- Agree or Disagree: In the end, love is God's answer to all of our conflicts.

- Reread Luke 23:34. What was the only loving recourse Jesus had left when his enemies had rejected all of his attempts to reach out to them? How can we apply this concept to our own lives?

- Reread Matthew 5:38-44. How do we try to justify getting revenge when an enemy has wronged us? How would you counsel a fellow Christian who is determined to satisfy his sinful need for vengeance?

- Read Luke 10:5. Brainstorm some new evangelism strategies that are based on the simple principle that Jesus articulated in this text.

Kids in Conflict

Let's turn the calendar back to a time when you were young. How long ago was it? Ten years? Twenty? Has it been 30 years? How much of your own childhood do you still remember? Do you recall some of the events that made your life back then so interesting, so challenging, so innocent, or so frightening? Can you remember when you had to deal with conflict—an argument with a parent, a bully's threats, a friend's words that hurt your feelings, or a stranger who wasn't very nice to you? Did you cry? Did you lash out in anger? Did you become aggressive and defend your turf or turn the other way and run?

Like adults, children have to learn how to deal with conflict. The sin that so often accompanies conflict generally comes quite naturally. But God wants his little ones to learn an approach to conflict that is distinctively different from the world's approach. He wants Christian children to grow in their understanding of how to cope with a hostile and sin-filled world. He wants them to behave in a way that will please him and show others what it means to be a child of God.

The following collection of conflict-resolution principles has been taken from God's Word, the Bible. The principles emphasize some of the more important points about dealing with conflict that God wants his children to know. Our purpose is to help Christian parents and teachers grasp the unique perspectives their children have on conflict and develop an approach to teaching these Bible truths in the most effective way.

When to Walk Away and When to Fight

Confrontational situations can quickly turn ugly. They can threaten a child's security and well-being. Kids need to know what their options are. Knowing when to flee and when to stand one's ground can be a difficult choice. In the heat of a tense moment, emotions are supercharged. Children often lack the maturity and experience to think these situations through. And they usually lack the presence of mind to remain calm so that they can carefully think through their response choices.

Some parents encourage their children to run away from a fight. This approach is mostly aimed at protecting their children from getting hurt. Other parents teach their kids to stand firm in the face of aggression. They know that there are bullies in the world who seek to control us. Their rationale is to teach their children to stand up to aggression early in life so that they will be well prepared when it happens in their adult years.

Scripture does not provide a simple formula for resolving this dilemma. While the Bible clearly teaches us to run away from temptation, fleeing sin is not always the same thing as running from a fight. There are times when we may have to fight for a just cause.

So, how can we help children when they find themselves face-to-face with conflict?

To begin, we can teach children to know the difference between defending oneself (or a neighbor) and striking back with an aggressive counterattack. The decision to counterattack crosses an invisible line that usually commits us to more conflict. Wise or unwise, once that decision has been made, the option to flee is effectively taken off the table. Kids need to know that.

It is also important to teach children to recognize tyranny when they see it. Bullying is unacceptable. But there are ways to confront a bully that do not have to lead to violence.

Look for teachable moments to discuss what bullying behaviors look like and why they are so dangerous. Walk children through hypothetical scenarios so they will know when standing up to a tyrant is appropriate. Explain that telling a responsible adult about bullying activity is an option that does not have to be seen as cowardly or vindictive.

The most dangerous thing about fighting is that it can damage our confidence and our trust in a God who wants us to come to him with all of our troubles. Children need to hear that message often.

The Don't-Let-the-Sun-Set-on-Your-Anger Principle

When someone wrongs us, anger is a common response. Anger has a way of growing from a molehill into a mountain. It can even degenerate into hatred.

The Bible tells us there is an urgency to resolving disputes sooner rather than later. Paul wrote, "'In your anger do not sin': Do not let the sun go down while you are still angry, and do not give the devil a foothold" (Ephesians 4:26,27). In other words, deal with it quickly—today, if possible. In this way, a bad situation won't escalate into something more dangerous and our confidence that God is in control will not be compromised.

God wants us to take the initiative in restoring peace to a relationship that has soured. In Matthew chapter 5 Jesus said, "If you are offering your gift at the altar and there remember that your brother has something against you, leave your gift there in front of the altar. First go and be reconciled to your brother; then come and offer your gift" (5:23,24).

A festering grudge is an open invitation to more discord. Children need to learn to make every effort to straighten things out, even when they may not have caused the conflict.

The Don't-Let-the-Sun-Set-on-Your-Anger Principle
God sees our conflicts and broken relationships as urgent. He wants us to seek healing and make reconciliation our highest priority (Ephesians 4:26; Matthew 5:22-24).

In worship we celebrate the peace we have with God. But we can only be truly joyful about that peace if we are also at peace with one another. So, it is important that we learn to address conflicts early. God only wants to see us at his altar when we have first made a genuine effort to restore and heal a broken relationship.

Finding the Strength to Do a Hard Thing

The Lord Jesus told us that we would have trouble in this world (John 16:33). Nobody likes to hear that, but it is a fact of life. Those of us who have children know that we would prefer to shield our children from this awful truth, at least until they are older and have had a chance to brace themselves for it. The truth is that most of our kids learn early on about conflict and the trouble it can cause. It is also true that most kids will learn about it the hard way. Some of their biggest troubles will involve the hurt that comes from relationships that have been ravaged by personal conflict.

How important it is, then, to teach them how to resolve their differences with others!

But this can be a difficult lesson. It requires strength to say to someone, "I'm sorry for being mean to you" or "I forgive you for the way you treated me, even if you aren't sorry."

The strength for doing something this difficult can only come from a loving and forgiving God who knows exactly how it feels to be treated with contempt and hatred.

In the model prayer that Jesus taught to his followers, he used the words, "Forgive us our debts, as we also forgive our debtors." It's a lesson all Christian parents will want their children to learn when they are very young. The power for actually doing such a hard thing comes from the faith we have in God, who promises to help us. Jesus once said that even a small amount of faith is enough to move a mountain because its power is found in God. If a little faith can accomplish something so impossible, it can also provide the inner strength to do the really hard things in life.

Thankfully, in addition to his promises to help us do the hard things in life, God also provides a simple tool for seeking his help. We call it prayer.

Prayer is a very powerful tool because it lets us come directly to our heavenly Father to ask for anything we need. With the gift of prayer, God gives us an opportunity to do something that is guaranteed to have an impact. God promises to hear our prayers and to answer them in a way that will benefit us. Parents will want to tell their children about this tool and practice using it on a daily basis. Kids need to know that at any time, in any situation, they can take full advantage of the powerful blessing of prayer.

The Plank-in-Your-Eye Principle

Kids can be cruel. Some children delight in finding fault with others and correcting them. By age 2, most children know that finger-pointing can put others in an unfavorable light, which, in turn, is an opportunity for them to occupy the more favorable light.

Jesus used a simple illustration to teach a basic truth about faultfinding and peacemaking. "Why do you look at the speck of sawdust in your brother's eye and pay no attention to the plank in your own eye? How can you say to your brother, 'Let me take the speck out of your eye,' when all the time there is a plank in your own eye? You hypocrite, first take the plank out of your own eye, and then you will see clearly to remove the speck from your brother's eye" (Matthew 7:3-5).

Jesus' Plank-in-Your-Eye Principle is a sobering reminder to deal first with the sin that lurks in our own lives. Only then will we have the right attitude for helping others deal with their sinful behaviors.

The Plank-in-Your-Eye Principle
Before you try to help another Christian deal with sin and temptation, make sure you recognize that you are also a sinner in need of God's forgiveness (Matthew 7:3-5).

This principle is easy enough to articulate. But teaching children to apply it to their own lives can require a lot of patience and understanding.

The issue is honesty. Kids would like to believe they never do anything wrong. Their young consciences have a hard time acknowledging the truth about the sin that contaminates their hearts. Children need to grow consciences that will be truthful and responsive to the presence of sin and guilt. They need to hear that their sins of omission are just as wrong as the sins they commit against others. And kids need to know that all of our wrongs have their origins in hearts that are already inclined to breaking God's commandments.

The unbelieving world opposes this notion. But God has given us all consciences just for the purpose of making us ever more aware of our guilt. Having active consciences is the only way we can become convinced that we really need a Savior from sin.

Parents and teachers can help children remove the planks in their eyes by holding them accountable for the wrong things they say and do. We can reinforce this concept by expecting children to verbally acknowledge their sins. Requiring a simple *I'm sorry* emphasizes the point. When a child is contrite, the heartwarming message that Jesus died to remove all of our guilt is the most positive reinforcement anyone can hear. A prayer thanking God for his tender mercy is an appropriate way to remember God's loving forgiveness and to be thankful for it.

Taking the plank out of our own eyes is a humbling process—one that places us directly at the foot of Jesus' cross. Moms, dads, and Christian educators will want to provide their humble, repentant lives as living examples of how to deal with the plank of sin.

The If-Your-Brother-Sins-Against-You Principle

Childhood is a beautiful thing. Adults are sad when the innocence of youth is gone. But let's not get carried away. It may be a hard fact to accept, but children are sinners just like their parents. Normally children do not commit felonies, but kids can be guilty of some mean-spirited behaviors. They lie, gossip, steal, and take part in a host of other misdemeanors.

The sins children commit against one another are frequently sins of aggression. We may think of them as the *early warning signs of future conflicts*. Like their adult counterparts, children obsess over the things they want. They distort the truth, judge one another, and punish those they see as deserving of their wrath.

The intervention plan that Jesus sketched for adults in Matthew 18:15-17 ("If your brother sins against you, . . .") sounds like it was tailor-made for kids. Most children understand how it feels to have a brother, a sister, or a classmate who has done something aimed at hurting them. Jesus' plan seems like a no-brainer for parents and Christian educators to teach to children. The steps are clear enough: (1) "Go and show him his fault, just between the two of you." (2) "If he will not listen, take one or two others along, so that 'every matter may be established by the testimony of two or three witnesses.'" (3) "If he refuses to listen to them, tell it to the church." And (4) "If he refuses to listen even to the church, treat him as you would a pagan or a tax collector." (For a child, telling it to the church may be problematic. Kids soon figure out that telling a parent or a teacher works better than firing off a letter to the Board of Elders. They also quickly come to the conclusion that social ostracizing can be sort of like treating a bully as a pagan or a tax collector.)

The If-Your-Brother-Sins-Against-You Principle

Out of love for a fellow Christian who has sinned against you, speak with him or her privately about this sin. If the individual remains unrepentant, take two or three other Christians with you to serve as witnesses. If the person still remains unrepentant, take the matter to the whole church and treat the individual as an unbeliever (Matthew 18:15-17). But keep this person in your prayers and look for opportunities to show that you still love and care about him or her.

But as simple as it may seem, there is a serious danger in training kids to follow the steps of Jesus' plan if we forget to include the most critical element. And what is that element? The critical element is the loving concern and compassion that serves as Jesus' underlying reason for sharing his plan with us in the first place. By following his plan yet ignoring its purpose, we would be turning a gospel-driven concern for sinners into a law-driven process that actually teaches kids to judge others. That is clearly not what Jesus intended.

Teach both *the plan* and *the purpose* for using the plan. Always remind children that when they are tempted to point out the sins of others, they must first look into their own hearts to find the motives behind their actions. They need to ask, *Why am I carrying out these steps?* If the answer is to get revenge or to make someone stop doing a hurtful thing to them, they are following Jesus' plan for the wrong reasons.

The Seven-Times-Seven Principle

If you've spent time with children, you've probably caught yourself saying something like, "How many times do I have to tell you to . . . ?" Whatever follows those words sounds worn out and hollow because you've said it so many times before. Kids seem to have a short memory when it comes to repeating the same dumb mistakes. We end up correcting them over and over.

Our kids are chips off the old blocks. How often don't we appear before our eternal Judge with a plea for mercy after repeating the same old sin for the umpteenth time? God's loving response is always the same: "You're forgiven, for Jesus' sake. Now go, and don't do it anymore." With God there is no limit to the number of times that we can be forgiven, even if it is for those sins that we repeat over and over.

When children find themselves caught up in a personal conflict with someone who continues to do the same mean things over and over, your constant reminders to forgive, and forgive, and forgive some more will begin to ring hollow and sound worn out. Your child's patience will begin to wear thin, just as your own patience can wear thin with your child, your neighbor, or your neighbor's children.

The Seven-Times-Seven Principle
Be patient with people who offend you. In Christian love, forgive them, even when they repeat the same sin over and over (Matthew 18:21,22).

Peter struggled with this same question. "How often do I have to forgive someone who keeps on offending me?" he asked. "Would seven times be a good hypothetical limit for me to set?"

Jesus suggested a different hypothetical number—one that would not be easy to keep track of. Forgive him *77* times. Better still, don't keep track of all the times you've had to say *I forgive you* to someone who has offended you.

You can still teach your child to add, "And please try not to do it again"—even if you doubt this will be the last time. Following Jesus means that we will not attach conditions to our forgiveness—this includes a statute of limitations on the number of times that we are ready to forgive. Children need to see their adult models living the same lesson in their lives.

[HINT: Read the parable that follows Jesus' words. It's found in Matthew 18:23-35. Then talk about how the parable applies to your child's life. Use specific examples from your child's own experience. And don't pass up the opportunity to consider how the parable applies to your life as well.]

The Forgive-and-Forget Principle

Children can be great little manipulators. It doesn't take long for kids to learn what works and what doesn't work in order to make things go their own way. One technique they will learn soon enough is to attach riders (or *conditions*) to their forgiveness as a way of leveraging their own agendas. Some may be able to figure out how to keep Mom or Dad feeling perpetually guilty about something. It becomes a great leveraging point. Others recognize they can keep friend and/or foe under their control by maintaining an ongoing list of wrongs that can be hauled out at a moment's notice whenever more pressure is needed.

Sometimes it is not enough just to teach a child to say, "I forgive you." For some it may be necessary to add the words, "I've already forgotten what you did to me."

> **The Forgive-and-Forget Principle**
> It's not enough to simply forgive someone who has wronged you. It is important also to forget about their offense and start your relationship over with a clean slate, just as God completely forgets our sins for Jesus' sake (Jeremiah 31:34).

Peacemaker Ministries has developed a four-part promise to help people let go of the sins that others have committed against them:

I will not dwell on this incident.

I will not bring this incident up again to use it against you.

I will not talk to others about this incident.

I will not let this incident stand between us or hinder our relationship.[224]

Get in the habit of praying the Lord's Prayer with your child every day. Talk about how these words fit the things that are going on in your child's life. Stop to think about the part of the prayer that asks God to "forgive us our sins, as we forgive those who sin against us." Spend a few minutes discussing what these words mean in real life.

The Rejoice-and-Restore Principle

We tend to forget to celebrate the blessings we have been given when enemies are able to reconcile and their hostility is brought to an end. Genuine unity is something to be savored and enjoyed. Peace is a gift from God, and he wants us to be good stewards of all of his gifts. A good steward is thankful for the gifts he has been given, and he says so to his benefactor. A good steward finds joy in putting the gifts to good use and not burying them out of sight. A good steward shares the gifts with others.

When children have worked their way through a personal conflict so that they can finally bring closure to a hostile relationship, we should not be too quick to pass over the event's significance. Take the time to acknowledge God's role in bringing former enemies together in a spirit of charity and forgiveness. Celebrate by saying a prayer of thanksgiving. Talk about the change of hearts that has occurred. Discuss the value of seeking peace when there is trouble in a relationship. And make sure that everyone recognizes that with peace comes full

The Rejoice-and-Restore Principle
When a brother or sister repents, the whole church rejoices in God's forgiveness and celebrates unity. The sinner is fully restored to his or her former status as a family member in God's household of faith (Luke 15:1-10).

reinstatement into God's family. Consider the example Jesus provided for us in Luke chapter 15 when he reinstated Peter into full discipleship.

The Turn-the-Other-Cheek Principle

One of the Bible's most difficult teachings for children to apply is the lesson about getting revenge. Not only does Jesus tell us that we are to resist the temptation to even the score with someone who has wronged us, but he also tells us that we are to demonstrate our love for the person who has just hit us and even pray for him or her. In the heat of battle, that's a very tall ideal to follow. Even mature Christians struggle with this concept.

When someone punches us in the face or hurts us with words that cut, the world's response is predictable: strike back, if for no other reason than as a deterrent. Make sure your enemy knows you will not stand still for getting hit again.

Jesus tells his followers to turn the other cheek instead. And he backed up this approach with his own living example. How easy it would have been for the Son of God to retaliate against the people who spit at him, drove thorns into his skull, and nailed him to a cross! Instead, he prayed for them, "Father, forgive them, for they do not know what they are doing" (Luke 23:34).

> **The Turn-the-Other-Cheek Principle**
> Do not retaliate against those who abuse you. Instead, treat a person who has abused you with kindness and generosity. And, in love, pray for that person (Matthew 5:39-44).

The Turn-the-Other-Cheek Principle is a hard teaching because it forces children to recognize that their faith in Jesus is also a call to stand tall in the face of danger and ridicule. That is a harsh reality. This teaching stands in stark contrast with the way the world would have us respond to injustice and aggression. Kids initially see Jesus' teaching as an unfair proposition. It just doesn't seem right.

This is a great time to talk about the great injustice of the sacrifice that Jesus made for us by dying in our place on Calvary's cross. He didn't deserve to be treated in this way. But he accepted it willingly for us because he loves us.

It is also a good time to teach children that Christianity is a radical call to personal self-sacrifice for Jesus, even as he sacrificed everything for them.

The Don't-Judge-Others Principle

In a child's world, the hard realities of life begin to set in very early—certainly much earlier than most parents would like to think. At a very early age, children have already begun to observe how many things are unfair.

Even the simplest of games have rules that need to be followed. It's not fair if someone wins because he has broken the rules and cheated to gain the victory. Nor is it fair if a referee, an umpire, a field judge, or a parent has made a bad call, giving a huge advantage to one's opponent. Most kids will tell you that if they could be the refs, their calls would always be fair. Put them to the test, and they would probably have some major difficulties with personal prejudices and biases.

The Don't-Judge-Others Principle
God does not want us to be the judges of the words, actions, or motives of other people (Matthew 7:1).

This desire to be the judge extends beyond childhood games. We are inclined to want to be the judge in real life as well. Some of us make an ongoing habit of trying to read the hearts and minds of others so that we may judge their motives as righteous or wicked.

The plain truth is that only God really knows what goes on in a person's heart.

While there are times and situations in which God gives a measure of authority to individuals who are called upon to serve as a kind of judge, he nevertheless remains the source and master of that authority. Those who are called upon to make judgments regarding the innocence or guilt of others (for example, governors, judges in the court system, teachers, or parents) do so because God has given them that authority. Such people are expected to carry out their God-given responsibility with great attention to being just and merciful in making their decision.

Helping children apply the Don't-Judge-Others Principle begins by teaching them about God's authority. As they get older, they will also learn how God shares his authority with some people for the sake of good order. The authority to judge others is restricted to those people to whom God has given such awesome responsibility. Beyond that, God does not want us to personally stand in judgment on anyone's behaviors or motives. Wrongfully judging others leads to conflict and disorder.

Five Smooth Stones

One of the small but beautiful wonders of Scripture is that God inspired its authors to occasionally divulge a curious detail for which no further explanation is offered. One such tantalizing piece of seemingly inconsequential information appears in the Old Testament story of David and Goliath.

As young David prepared to face the enemy's giant in mortal combat, we are told that he "took his staff in his hand, chose five smooth stones from the stream, put them in the pouch of his shepherd's bag and, with his sling in his hand, approached the Philistine" (1 Samuel 17:40). We have no idea why the ancient writer (Samuel) felt compelled to tell us that David chose "five smooth stones." What follows is my own idea about how those five smooth stones can be put to good use as a memory aid for summarizing the attitude of a peacemaking warrior in the church militant.

STONE ONE: **Faith.** God is faithful; trust his promises. Faith sets a Christian's approach to conflict resolution apart from secular conflict-resolution strategies. Your confidence that God will provide the resources you need to accomplish the impossible empowers you.

STONE TWO: **Humility.** Search your heart. Be prepared to repent of your own sins. Where you have wronged your neighbor, acknowledge it and ask your neighbor to forgive you. Then look to the cross of Christ for God's forgiveness and healing.

STONE THREE: **Forgiveness.** Forgive those who have hurt you, even as God has forgiven you. God's selfless love motivates you to forgive others unconditionally. Be patient and long-suffering for the sake of those whose faith is weak or fragile, even when their words and behaviors remain belligerent.

STONE FOUR: **God's Promises.** Among Christians the common ground for dialog is the Bible, where God promises to give you his power to heal broken relationships. The Bible is the source of truth, hope, encouragement, and comfort. Look for opportunities to read and study Scripture together with people who are in conflict with you.

STONE FIVE: **Prayer.** The unbelieving world will hate Christians and act like an enemy. Unbelievers may not be willing to dialog or respond to sincere overtures for peace. Ask God to forgive them when they damage your reputation or harm your body. Seek God's strength to endure in the face of their attacks. Pray for the wisdom to remember that your real enemy is Satan and his evil angels.

Endnotes

Introduction

[1] Colossians 1:19,20.

[2] Some scholars think that the word *Jerusalem* comes from the Hebrew words *Jeru Shalom,* which mean "City of Peace."

[3] A similar plea appears in Philippians 2:1-5, where Paul encouraged the Christians living in Philippi to set their egos aside and make every effort to be "one in spirit and purpose."

[4] Isaiah 53:3-6.

[5] All of their relationships, no doubt, were a reflection of the absolute harmony and ineffable unity that already existed within the mysterious relationship of the Trinity.

[6] This is an intriguing detail. Adam and Eve had no previous experience with war or the tools of war.

[7] Genesis 3:24.

[8] Matthew 5:9.

Chapter 1: Sin That Entangles

[9] Philippians 1:3-6.

[10] Alfred Poirier, *The Peacemaking Pastor: A Biblical Guide to Resolving Church Conflict* (Grand Rapids: Baker Books, 2006).

[11] We will later refer to this kind of work as *intervention ministry* or *peacemaking.*

[12] Galatians 6:1.

[13] Human conflict can, in fact, be the result of sins committed against any of the commandments in the Second Table of God's Law.

[14] Genesis 4:7.

Chapter 2: Predictable Patterns

[15] Poirier, pp. 57-59. Poirier uses an interesting anecdote to make his point. "One night after dinner I called my wife and my children to family worship. I went to get my Bible and when I returned, I was struck by the look of boredom in their faces and the sense of resistance and disrespect communicated in their body language. Through all this, I ignored them and began as a dutiful father to do the right thing—or so I thought. I read Scripture, asked questions, and proceeded to hear the lamest of responses. I became angry and eventually erupted. 'What's the matter with you? Don't you love God? This is God's Word. What's wrong with you?' No sooner were the words out of my mouth than the Holy Spirit convicted me. My desire for family worship was mixed with a desire for self-worship, the self-worship won out. I demanded a show of respect. I damned my family for not giving it to me. Above all, I erected and served a god in the very place where we were meant to worship our Savior."

[16] Matthew 26:42.

Chapter 3: A Case Study

[17] Proverbs 27:17.

[18] Ephesians 4:29.

[19] Ephesians 4:21-25.

[20] Armin J. Panning wrote, "Far from accepting false doctrine, spiritually mature Christians will rather go on the offensive against it. They will '[speak] the truth in love.' . . . It is important that such speakers not only be correct (speak the truth) but also that they speak 'in love.' They are not to lord it over their weaker brothers. Nor are they viciously to turn on false teachers but, rather, to speak as lovingly and as winsomely as possible in the hope of winning over the proponent of an incorrect view. Then the unity will be kept, and growth in the church will be effected." (*Galatians, Ephesians,* of The People's Bible series [Milwaukee: Northwestern Publishing House, 2000], p. 186.)

Chapter 4: The Need to Justify

[21] Genesis 3:7-13.

[22] In *A Commentary on Genesis 1–11,* by Carl J. Lawrenz and John C. Jeske (Milwaukee: Northwestern Publishing House, 2004, pp. 141-143), we read, "Adam and Eve revealed their depraved condition. [They] vainly sought to hide from God, vainly sought to protect [themselves] from God's just punishment with [their] own feeble and foolish efforts. Here is the beginning of the *opinio legis,* man's vain thought of somehow rescuing and saving himself from God's punishment. This opinion of the law has remained indelibly ingrained in natural man ever since. . . . Vainly [they] sought refuge in half-truths, deceit, and evasion. . . . What a disgraceful confession Adam made as he tried to blame others, to blame Eve, and ultimately to blame God himself! Where trust in God is gone, there is also no love of God; and where there is no love for God, real unselfish love for one's neighbor also fades away."

[23] *The Anatomy of Peace: Resolving the Heart of Conflict,* The Arbinger Institute (n.p.: Berrett-Koehler Publishers, 2008), p. 112.

[24] Leviticus 5:17; Proverbs 11:19.

[25] Exodus chapter 20.

[26] Such behaviors are embraced in the last seven of God's Ten Commandments. A quick review of the Second Table of the Law demonstrates how pervasive conflict really is. Serious conflict can grow out of the sins that any one of these last seven commandments addresses.

Chapter 5: High Ground, Slippery Slopes, and Bottomlands

[27] Ken Sande, *The Peacemaker: A Biblical Guide to Resolving Personal Conflict,* Third Ed. (n.p.: Baker Books, 2004).

[28] It may be a minor point, but this author would prefer to reverse the relative positions for *assault* and *litigation* on Sande's illustration.

[29] Here a distinction will need to be made between murder and the kind of killing that goes on when countries are at war. It is possible to be a warrior, fully engaged in destroying an enemy, but still have a heart that is at peace. Murder, on the other hand, is the implicit behavior of a heart that is at war. Jesus said that it was a sin just to *think* hateful and murderous thoughts about an enemy. The case of Samson in Judges chapter 16 always raises some interesting questions with regard to both murder and suicide. But in Samson's

case, we need to remember that this event was occurring during an ongoing war with a heathen nation, which God himself had said must be expelled from the Promised Land. Samson died, honoring God's will.

[30] Matthew 23:1-39.

[31] Galatians 6:7.

[32] Eviatar Zerubavel, *The Elephant in the Room: Silence and Denial in Everyday Life* (New York: Oxford University Press, 2006).

[33] 1 John 1:8a.

[34] 1 John 1:8-10.

[35] Colossians 3:1,5-10.

[36] Robert E. Pittenger, *The First Five Minutes: A Sample of Microscopic Interview Analysis* (Ithica, New York: Paul Martineau, 1960).

[37] Eviatar Zerubavel, *The Elephant in the Room: Silence and Denial in Everyday Life* (New York: Oxford University Press, 2006).

[38] "Gotta Have Faith," *New York Times*, December 17, 2002.

[39] Jill Hastings and Marion Typpo, *An Elephant in the Living Room: A Leader's Guide for Helping Children of Alcoholics* (Center City, MN: Hazelden Publishing, 1984).

[40] Eviatar Zerubavel, "Social Mindscapes," unpublished manuscript.

[41] The meaning for the Eighth Commandment, Luther's Small Catechism, Gauzewitz Edition.

[42] See Jeremiah 6:14.

[43] James C. Humes, *The Wit and Wisdom of Abraham Lincoln: A Treasury of Quotations, Anecdotes, and Observations* (New York: Gramercy Books, 1996).

[44] Everett C. Hughes, "Good People and Dirty Work," from *The Sociological Eye: Selected Papers* (New Brunswick: Transaction Books, 1971).

Chapter 6: On Earth Peace to Men

[45] Philippians 1:5.

[46] From the text of hymn 54, "Where Shepherds Lately Knelt," by Jaroslav J. Vajda, *Christian Worship* (Milwaukee: Northwestern Publishing House, 1993).

Chapter 7: The Gathering Storm

[47] Attributed to James Q. Wilson, Pepperdine University, from *The Wall Street Journal,* February 15, 2006.

[48] 1 Corinthians 16:14; 1 Corinthians 13:4-7.

[49] Lange writes, "Critical, fault-finding judgments are not the way of love. Love puts the best interpretation on the actions of others. Rather than thinking or speaking evil of our neighbor, we will defend him and speak well of him. If someone is ensnared by false doctrine, we will then admonish the person in love." (*God So Loved the World: A Study of Christian Doctrine* [Milwaukee: Northwestern Publishing House, 2005], page 413.)

[50] *The Anatomy of Peace: Resolving the Heart of Conflict,* The Arbinger Institute (n.p.: Berrett-Koehler Publishers, 2008), p. 186.

[51] Matthew 28:18; John 19:11.

[52] John 1:14.

[53] Isaiah 53:10.

[54] Mark 8:31.

[55] John 19:30.

[56] Hosea 13:14.

[57] Romans 8:28-39.

Chapter 8: The Peacemaker's Calling

[58] Matthew 5:3-11.

[59] Matthew 5:1,2.

[60] Romans 8:28-37.

[61] Romans 5:1,2.

[62] 1 Peter 1:15,16.

[63] David Valleskey, *2 Corinthians,* from The People's Bible series (Milwaukee: Northwestern Publishing House, 2000), p. 93.

[64] Romans 5:10.

[65] Matthew 5:13.

[66] Matthew 5:14-16.

[67] Luke 13:20,21.

[68] Ephesians 4:11-13; 1 Peter 1:1,2.

[69] David P. Scaer, *Discourses in Matthew: Jesus Teaches the Church* (St. Louis: Concordia Publishing House, 2004), pp. 216ff.

[70] Psalm 23:1.

[71] 2 Corinthians 10:5.

[72] Ibid. Scaer, p. 220.

[73] Matthew 16:24.

[74] Ephesians 5:1,2.

[75] Hebrews 12:2.

[76] 1 Corinthians 12:12-30; Romans 12:6.

[77] Colossians 4:5,6.

[78] Daniel M. Deutschlander, *The Theology of the Cross: Reflections on His Cross and Ours* (Milwaukee: Northwestern Publishing House, 2008), pp. 144,145.

Chapter 9: Conflict and Faith

[79] Matthew 9:20-22.

[80] Matthew 15:21-28.

[81] Matthew 8:5-10.

[82] Matthew 8:23-26.

[83] Matthew 14:22-31.

[84] Matthew 17:14-21; Mark 9:14-29.

[85] Matthew gives us a sense of this discussion's potential for fanning the flames of conflict. In chapter 20 the apostle reports that the mother of James and John asked Jesus to give her sons places of great honor in his kingdom. Then

Matthew adds that some of the other disciples were indignant over her request. They were angry about the arrogance and injustice of the woman's request. As long as they failed to see things from God's perspective, the conversation about great faith would remain a potentially explosive topic. Mark reports that when Jesus asked his disciples what they were arguing about on the road, they "kept quiet because on the way they had argued about who was the greatest" (Mark 9:33,34).

[86] Genesis 11:1-9.

[87] Titus 3:3; Romans 5:10.

[88] 1 Timothy 1:13.

[89] Matthew 17:20,21.

Chapter 10: The Marks of a Peacemaker

[90] Matthew 7:3-5.

[91] *The Anatomy of Peace: Resolving the Heart of Conflict,* The Arbinger Institute (n.p.: Berrett-Koehler Publishers, 2008), pp. 217ff.

[92] John Jackson and Lorraine Bossé-Smith, *Leveraging Your Leadership Style* (Nashville: Abingdon Press, 2007), p. 20.

[93] Isaiah 43:22ff.

[94] Matthew 10:21,22.

[95] Attributed to C. S. Lewis.

[96] Matthew 28:20.

[97] J. P. Meyer, "The Image of God, Genesis 1," unpublished essay, p. 5.

[98] Isaiah 54:10.

[99] 1 Timothy 1:13.

[100] 1 Corinthians 16:13.

Chapter 11: Power Tools for Peacemakers

[101] Ephesians 4:2.

[102] 1 Timothy 2:5; Galatians 3:20.

[103] John 14:6.

[104] Leviticus 22:14. The leftovers from certain sacrificial offerings were designated as part of the priests' income. If someone accidentally forgot this and ate meat that rightfully belonged to the priests, fair compensation, plus a smaller percentage, was required as restitution. This is a biblical example of compensatory law.

[105] 1 Peter 1:22; 1 Corinthians 13.

[106] Colossians 3:13.

[107] Matthew 6:12.

[108] Attributed to W. Steven Brown as quoted in *Speaker's Sourcebook II,* by Glen Van Ekeren (n.p.: Prentice Hall Press, 1993), p. 71.

[109] Romans 12:10.

[110] John 13:3-17.

[111] Douglas Stone, Bruce Patton, Sheila Heen, *Difficult Conversations: How to Discuss What Matters Most,* The Harvard Negotiation Project (n.p.: Penguin Books,

1999), pp. 17ff.

[112] Ibid, pp. 18,19.

[113] Romans 12:10.

[114] 2 Timothy 2:15.

[115] Ephesians 4:15,16.

[116] Fyodor Dostoevsky, *The Idiot,* 1869.

[117] Genesis 29–32.

[118] Genesis 28:10-22.

[119] Hymn 411:1. *Christian Worship* (Milwaukee: Northwestern Publishing House, 1993).

[120] Luke 11:10-13.

[121] Psalm 46:8-10; Matthew 10:29-31.

[122] Genesis 3:7-10.

[123] Luther's Large Catechism, *Concordia Triglotta,* 753:84; *The Book of Concord,* ed. Theodore G. Tappert, 446:84.

Chapter 12: Talkin' Strategy

[124] In *The Shepherd Under Christ,* by Armin W. Schuetze and Irwin J. Habeck (Northwestern Publishing House, 1974, p. 169), we read, "Brotherly admonition ought to have only one purpose, that of reclaiming a sinning brother for his own spiritual good and for the glory of the Lord and his church. It ought never to be . . . undertaken to give the offender a tongue lashing for the irritation which he has caused, or to parade one's own superiority. Above all its purpose must not be simply to get rid of a troublesome member. The attitude in which it is to be exercised is to be one of meekness and humility, recognizing one's own weakness and sinfulness, and yearning to help a fallen brother even as one would want his brother to help him if the situation were reversed (Gal 6:1)."

[125] Victor H. Prange, *Luke,* from The People's Bible series (Milwaukee: Northwestern Publishing House, 1988).

[126] Romans 14:19.

[127] In Matthew 7:24-27 Jesus uses the illustration of a wise builder who builds on the foundation of his Word. The choice he makes of building on a foundation of solid rock so that the house can withstand the storms describes a proactive style of ministry that prepares people for the challenges to their faith that will most certainly come.

[128] In Galatians 6:1 the apostle Paul describes an approach to ministry that is more of a ministry reaction or response to helping someone who is caught in the eye of one of those personal storms of life. That is what makes it a reactive ministry.

[129] Luke 17:5; Romans 1:11,12; Philemon 4-7.

[130] 1 Thessalonians 5:14; Galatians 6:1; James 5:19,20.

[131] 2 Timothy 4:2; Philippians 3:12-14.

[132] Genesis 6:11-13.

[133] Genesis 9:12-17.

[134] Jesus' plan, recorded in Matthew 18:15ff., begins with the words, "If your brother sins against you, . . ." The Greek word translated "against" *(eis)* is a

multipurpose preposition that in Greek has many meanings. It is one of the most frequently used words in the Greek language. A rationale attempting to limit the kinds of sin Jesus was here referring to as sins of conflict would be out of order. His point is that if someone cheated you in a business dealing, moved a boundary stone, used dishonest scales, slandered you, stirred up conflict, etc., this is how you should deal with him.

[135] Matthew 18:12-14.

[136] 1 Corinthians 4:21.

[137] Ephesians 4:32.

[138] Matthew 18:18-20.

[139] John 4:4-42.

[140] Matthew 9:9,10.

[141] Proverbs 15:22.

[142] Quoted from the consultation agreement used by Ambassadors of Reconciliation from Billings, Montana—an intervention service connected with the Lutheran Church—Missouri Synod.

[143] 1 Thessalonians 1:4-10.

[144] The intervention strategy proposed in the Arbinger Institute's secular book *The Anatomy of Peace: Resolving the Heart of Conflict* (2008) makes *relationship building with influential people* a major part of the conflict-resolution objectives. This is also a critical element in family intervention strategies: "If we want to be a positive influence with your child, we better have a strong relationship with you. . . . Parents must [learn how] to build relationships with those who have influence with their children, beginning with their spouses, or former spouses for that matter" (p. 210).

[145] Hebrews 12:2,3; Matthew 28:18-20.

[146] 1 Thessalonians 1:2,3.

Chapter 13: The Most Excellent Way

[147] 1 John 3:16; John 15:12.

[148] John 3:30.

[149] 2 Samuel 12.

[150] Psalm 32:5. In 2 Samuel chapter 12 we have an example of both confession and absolution as David admits, "I have sinned against the LORD," and Nathan replies, "The LORD has taken away your sin. You are not going to die."

[151] Psalm 32:5; Psalm 41:4.

[152] Luther said that there are two parts to this process: *confession* and *absolution*. Confession acknowledges our sins; absolution is a proclamation that all of our sins are absolved or forgiven. *Christian Worship* contains an excellent order for Private Confession on pages 154-155. By the author's own unscientific observation, it would appear that the process is rarely used. Church leaders may want to consider practical ways to reinvigorate the *Lutheran* practice of private confession and absolution among God's people.

[153] Matthew 19:16-22.

[154] See Matthew 18:23-35. In this parable of the unmerciful servant, Jesus teaches us to consider how God has dealt with our sin. God's forgiveness is a never-ending fountain, constantly flowing to us. This is the standard that God

expects forgiven sinners to apply to their own relationships when others sin against us.

[155] 1 Chronicles 28:9.

[156] Jeremiah 31:34. Also see Hebrews 9:22-28 for a word picture that adds insight regarding our loving God's sacrifice, which was made on our behalf.

[157] Matthew 24:9-12.

[158] Attributed to C. S. Lewis.

Chapter 14: A City of Peace

[159] John 16:10.

[160] John 16:17.

[161] Isaiah 50:7; Luke 18:31-34.

[162] Psalm 133:1-3, a song of ascents by David.

[163] Luke 22:24.

[164] Luke 9:46-48; Matthew 20:20-28.

[165] Luke 22:24-30.

[166] 1 Peter 5:5,6.

[167] *Bible History Commentary: New Testament, Volume 1,* Werner H. Franzmann, WELS Board for Parish Education, 1989, pp. 732-740. Franzmann goes on to say that Jesus is here restating "the matter of true greatness among his followers. . . . He is pointing to believers whom others in the church willingly recognize and follow as their leaders. And all such leaders in the church will be great in the eyes of God only when they lead their fellow believers in the spirit and in the manner of lowly servants."

[168] Ibid, page 740.

[169] John 15:18–16:4.

[170] Ephesians 2:19-22.

[171] John 13:1; see Franzmann, p. 735.

[172] John 15:4.

[173] John 15:16.

[174] John 13:34,35; John 15:17.

[175] John 16:27.

[176] John 17:11.

[177] John 17:23.

[178] Galatians 3:26ff.

[179] 1 Corinthians 1:17; Galatians 3:28; Ephesians 4:13.

[180] One strategic approach to resolving conflict that has proven effective is the concept of *détente*—an agreed-upon period of time when hostilities are relaxed or suspended between conflicted parties in the hope that the cooling-down process will lead to a resolution.

[181] 1 Corinthians 1:27-29.

[182] 2 Corinthians 12:7-10.

[183] Philippians 4:13.

[184] John 16:23,24.

[185] Ezekiel 11:19.

[186] Romans 6:17,18.

[187] Colossians 3:15-17.

[188] Mark 14:22-24; Luke 22:19,20.

[189] Luke 22:19b; Acts 2:42.

[190] Matthew 28:18-20.

[191] John 21:15-17.

[192] Psalm 34:1-14.

[193] Hebrews 13:17.

[194] See Genesis 14:18-20; Hebrews 5:4-6 and 7:1-28. Melchizedek worshiped the same true God that Abram worshiped. The Old Testament describes him as the "king of Salem" ("king of peace") and a "priest of God Most High" (Jeske, *Genesis,* from The People's Bible series, p. 136). In New Testament times, however, Israel's priestly order was fulfilled in Jesus, the ultimate High Priest, who sacrificed himself on the altar of the cross for us. John Jeske writes, "He is the one and only priest who can make things right with God." That is why Pastor Teschendorf directed Stan and Mark to stand at the foot of Christ's cross above the altar. That is where we all need to go when sins remain unresolved or unaddressed in our hearts. By bringing them together under the shadow of the cross, Pastor Teschendorf was acting out his role as God's ambassador of peace. Jesus Christ (represented by the cross) is our mediator with God. By bringing Mark and Stan together before the cross, Tim Teschendorf was bringing them both to their mediator, Christ, to begin making their peace with each other. And he was not acting in this role specifically as a function of his pastoral office but rather as a peacemaker in God's army of believers. You and I are foot soldiers in that same army. We have been called to serve as his peacemakers—members of a royal priesthood of all believers (1 Peter 2:9).

[195] Matthew 3:16,17; John 19:30; Philippians 1:3-6.

[196] Matthew 5:23,24; Ephesians 5:2.

[197] The Old Testament tells us about a sacrifice God designated as the fellowship offering. The traditional term that was used for this offering was peace offering. The Pentateuch (especially Exodus, Leviticus, and Numbers) refers often to these sacrificial offerings. The peace offering is linked to some of the topics that we have discussed in this book: enmity, hostility, fellowship with God and one another, celebration, and the like.

Chapter 15: Coals of Fire

[198] John 15:17; John 13:34,35.

[199] 2 Corinthians 5:14; 2 Timothy 3:16 and 4:2; 1 Timothy 6:3-5.

[200] 1 Corinthians 4:6-21. Note: The apostle Paul ends this section with the question, "What do you prefer? Shall I come to you with a whip, or in love and with a gentle spirit?"

[201] In "Selections From a Genesis Commentary" (*Wisconsin Lutheran Quarterly,* Vol. 78, No. 4, p. 10), Carl J. Lawrenz wrote, "St. John closes the section (1 John 3:11-15) with an exhortation: 'Do not be surprised, my brothers, if the world hates you.' . . . It began with Cain's hatred of Abel, and it is experienced by Christians today. It is not that Christians hate the unbelievers as persons. . . . The hostility arises from the unbelieving world which remains

adamant in its sin and unbelief. The unbelievers, Satan's seed, resent the Christians' childlike trust in their Savior and the loving, thankful service which the Christians render to their God and Savior in such humble faith."

[202] John 18:1-11.

[203] Galatians 3:26,27.

[204] Revelation 1:17,18.

[205] 1 Peter 5:8,9.

[206] "Eve had become the willing servant of Satan. She obeyed his lie. She had announced her trust in God and hence had withdrawn also her obedience to God. . . . Satan was rejoicing. . . . God, however, announced 'Enmity, hostility will I establish between you and the woman. . . .' We also saw how man had displayed enmity toward the woman, blaming her for her transgression. But all this enmity and hostility was misdirected. If man was to be helped, this enmity would have to be redirected in the proper direction again . . . and his enmity would again have to be directed upon Satan. . . . Proper enmity would have to be established by his divine initiative. It could be established in no other way." ("Selections From a Genesis Commentary" [Carl J. Lawrenz, *Wisconsin Lutheran Quarterly*, Vol. 78, No. 4, p. 9]).

[207] 2 Corinthians 10:4; Psalm 44:5; Luke 10:19.

[208] We may also take comfort in Luther's "A Mighty Fortress Is Our God," in which the reformer writes,

> Though devils all the world should fill,
> All eager to devour us,
> We tremble not, we fear no ill;
> They shall not overpow'r us.
> This world's prince may still
> Scowl fierce as he will,
> He can harm us none.
> He's judged; the deed is done!
> One little word can fell him.
>
> Hymn 200, *Christian Worship* (Milwaukee: Northwestern Publishing House, 1993).

[209] *Bible History Commentary: New Testament, Volume 1*, Werner H. Franzmann, WELS Board for Parish Education, 1989, p. 734. (See also John 6:70,71; 13:2,21,26-30; 18:2-5.)

[210] Luke 22:35,36.

[211] Matthew 10:16ff.

[212] When immigrants seek American citizenship, they are required to repeat an Oath of Allegiance to the United States of America, which, in part, reads, "I will support and defend the Constitution of the United States of America against all enemies, foreign and domestic [and] bear arms on behalf of the United States." Lyle Lange writes, "Government has the right to wage war against an aggressor nation to protect its citizens. Our Lutheran Confessions state, 'Christians may without sin . . . wage just wars; serve as soldiers' (AC XVI:2 [German text]). . . . Pacifists err when they say that all war is wrong. . . . They err . . . when they try to apply Jesus' words in the Sermon on the Mount to government (Mt 5:38-48). Government cannot maintain order by turning the other cheek. It is charged by God to use force to protect its citizens. Christians, then, may serve in wars with a clear conscience, for they are acting as agents of the government." (Lyle W. Lange, *God So Loved the World: A Study of Christian Doctrine* [Milwaukee, Northwestern Publishing House, 2005], p. 656.)

[213] See Matthew 7:1.

[214] One biblical example that demonstrates the sinner's instinct for vengeance is recorded in Judges 16:21-30. In verse 21 we learn that the Philistines gouged out the eyes of a captive Samson. Later, as Samson approached his final act, he asked God to give him strength one more time to "get revenge on the Philistines for my two eyes" (verse 28). Apparently, while making the ultimate sacrifice to bring glory and honor to the true God, Samson could not ignore his personal desire for some final payback for what these enemies had done to him.

[215] Isaiah 53:4-7.

[216] 1 Peter 2:20; Matthew 5:11; Romans 5:3; Romans 8:17,18.

[217] Romans 12:19.

[218] Deuteronomy 32:35.

[219] Luke 23:34.

[220] Matthew 28:20.

[221] Romans 12:14; Romans 14:19.

[222] Hebrews 12:14.

[223] Luke 10:5.

Appendix A: Kids in Conflict

[224] Ken Sande, *The Peacemaker: A Biblical Guide to Resolving Personal Conflict* (n.p.: Baker Books, 2004).